T0419498

Enchanted Strings

BOB BAKER MARIONETTE THEATER

Marionettes from *Over the Garden Wall*. Most of these marionettes stand only about two feet tall.

Enchanted Strings

BOB BAKER MARIONETTE THEATER

Randal J. Metz

FOREWORD BY

Jordan Peele

Happy the Birthday Dog greets a young child celebrating her birthday—as evidenced by the "solid gold adjustable crown" presented to her.

This book is dedicated to the children of Los Angeles, and the child within us all.

Bob Baker poses with a waltzer on the stage of the theater's original location in the Echo Park neighborhood near downtown Los Angeles.

BOB BAKER MARIONETTES

Nearly a half century of innovation in style and scale was on display backstage at a Bob Baker show.

Foreword by Jordan Peele

The lights dim. There's a hush. Crying stops. Phones turn off. Humans dressed like the backdrop take the stage. There's a brief welcome. The lights go out. The music begins. The crowd becomes an audience. And we are rapt.

The objects come out, one act at a time.

There is something that happens to me when I watch great puppetry. A tickle in the back of my spine. Doesn't really matter how grumpy, tired, or distracted I am . . . it doesn't even matter if I haven't had my coffee. In those first moments when the puppeteer fades and the puppet comes alive, I do too. I'm in. I buy it. In fact, I don't just believe, I want to believe. What once was inanimate is now alive, and all my cynical tendencies are forgotten. Traded in, so I can be four again.

There was a period in my life when all I wanted to do was make puppets—not as a hobby but as a livelihood. I went to Sarah Lawrence College for two years with the intended goal of studying this craft and becoming a puppeteer. All because of the wonder that puppetry brings.

During this time, the most fascinating thing I learned about puppeteering was that the puppets themselves, despite being inanimate, are not innocent bystanders in the craft. They command respect. They take discipline and ingenuity to build them. And a relinquishing of control to operate them. You can build a puppet out of anything, even a dirty sock, but after you craft something you have to listen carefully to it. A good puppeteer has to pay attention to what it wants to be. What type of personality does it have? What does it want to do? Can it sing? Is it funny? Is it mean? If you string a bunch of objects together and hang them from another object, they will hang a certain way because of gravity. And so a puppet isn't so much "operated," it's guided into being.

It's more than the act, the comedy the puppet performs, or the song it sings, it's the soul of the thing itself that has me captivated. The marionette, a noble breed, demands respect of the audience and its puppeteer as well. Defiant and graceful, loose and exact. To witness a presence born of string and gravity is miraculous. The illusion can wander from silly to spooky, sweet to sultry. Doesn't matter. It all seems to resonate on a deeper level. We are our connections.

And once I've bought in, I can't unsee it. And that's what tickles me most. A puppet doesn't become an object again after the show's over. It just goes to sleep. Once it gets life, you can't take it away. It's a reassuring notion.

I've visited the Bob Baker Marionette Theater numerous times, and each time the experience feels completely new. Throughout its history, the theater has amassed an amazing, intricate roster of puppets, deepest I've ever seen. Each one is unique, and alive, and sleeping until the next show. I hope you enjoy exploring this world the Bob Baker artists have created.

Introduction: The Magic of Puppets

I first fell under the magic spell of puppetry when I was ten years old and visited Children's Fairyland in Oakland, California. Fairyland opened in 1950 and is home to the Storybook Puppet Theater, which debuted in 1956, making it the oldest continuously running puppet theater in the United States. While there, I witnessed Lewis Mahlmann's production of *Treasure Island*. The puppets came alive and, for the first time, I was drawn into the magic of theater. At that moment, I decided to become a puppeteer. In the ignorance of my youth, I knocked on the door of the theater and offered Mahlmann one dollar for each of his puppets. (After all, puppets only cost a dollar in the city of Tijuana, Mexico.) Mahlmann didn't slam the door in my face. Instead, he opened it. He offered me the chance to come back anytime and learn the art that I cherished so much. He became my first and primary mentor. From that day on, I began working for Fairyland and, in my free time, studying theater and puppetry.

Flash ahead twelve years. While pursuing my theater arts degree, I often traveled in the summers, performing "Punch and Judy" and the masked Italian theatrical form *commedia dell'arte*. I knew of Bob Baker and his theater, and had seen him perform a couple of times at annual puppeteers' conventions. (Yes—there are annual conventions for puppeteers, held each year by the non-profit group Puppeteers of America.) One weekend, fate brought us together. Bob and his assistant, Tom Ray, were performing at the Humboldt County Fair alongside my own puppet company. I was overjoyed to be on the same bill as Bob. As it turned out, as much as I loved Bob's show, he liked mine, too. On the last day of the fair, he pulled me aside and offered me a job at his marionette theater anytime I wanted. I was on cloud nine, though I actually thought he might have just been being nice. My place was with Fairyland and the Storybook Theater.

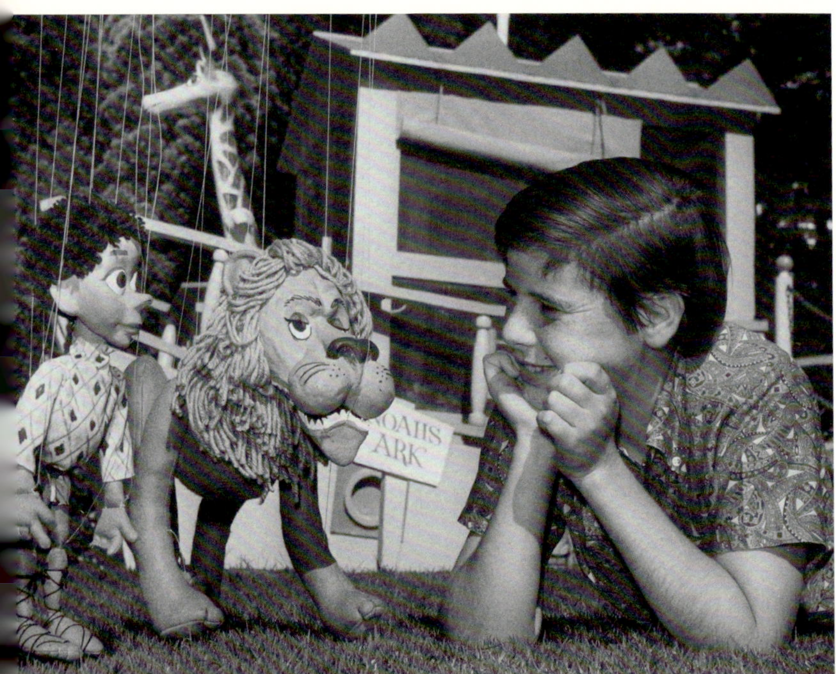

By 1985, I had graduated from San Francisco State University and was the artistic director for Fairyland. The executive director thought I should pursue any chances I had for expanding my puppet knowledge. She knew Mahlmann wanted me to take over the puppet theater eventually. At the time, I was very interested in learning the style of marionette work done by Bob's company. At Fairyland, we only performed with the classical style of hands, rods, and marionettes. Bob's shows were presented in a nightclub revue form, using large, colorful marionettes.

After a quick correspondence with Bob, he hired me at the beginning of 1986. Between 1986 and

1990, I traveled back and forth from the Bay Area to Los Angeles, learning the art of marionettes from the master himself. Bob became my second mentor in puppetry. Fairyland wouldn't let me leave completely, so I was living in L.A. and designing for the park while also working at Bob's side. Before I left the Bay Area, Mahlmann handed me a large wrapped box. Inside, I found all the marionettes for *Treasure Island*. He didn't want me to forget my roots. For the two years I lived in Los Angeles, they hung in my apartment as a reminder of why I wanted to be a puppeteer.

By that point, I was completely engulfed in the magic. When I was not onstage performing puppetry with puppet artists King Hall and Roy Raymond, I was in the workshop working closely with Bob and John Leland on all their projects. I will never forget the lessons I learned there. When my day was over, I remained with Bob while he toiled late into the night, watching him as he worked and, in his folksy way, spun tales of life in Hollywood, collaborations with Disney, and our crazy artistic world. This was a once-in-a-lifetime internship, and I wasn't going to miss a moment of it. In 1988, I returned to Children's Fairyland to work full time, and to marry my fiancée I'd left behind. But once or twice a year, I returned to Bob's to help with work, perform traveling Christmas shows, and learn to pull new strings.

In 2020, I celebrated my fiftieth year as a professional puppeteer. Although I won't be able to recount everything I learned, my goal in these pages is to tell Bob's story the way he told it to me. Bob always wanted to open a puppet school in conjunction with the marionette theater. Unfortunately, that dream never came to pass. But, in a way, he *has* opened his school. The men and women who worked with Bob are part of the success of this magical place. He trained them—and they trained him. Bob would always say that the day you stopped learning was the day to hang up the puppets.

The greatest gift Bob gave to the people of Los Angeles was the new generation of puppeteers who have carried on his tradition since he passed in 2014. They have worked his magic to rebuild this historic cultural landmark. The theater is once again giving young puppeteers a place to perform, learn, and create. Their mission: to educate, celebrate, and inspire imagination through puppetry and the allied arts.

By telling the history of Bob's theater, I can keep Bob's dream alive for everyone. I still remember his words to me as I left to go back home: "Return whenever you like, and share the knowledge I passed to you." And now, sit back . . . relax . . . and enjoy the artistry, history, and magic of the Bob Baker Marionette Theater!

Randal Metz was enchanted by puppets at a very early age, and would eventually build his own creations (right).

Bob Baker Marionette Theater unpacking into the York Theatre, filling the 1923 vaudeville stage with marionettes, scenery, and magic.

COTTON CLUB
The BROWN DERBY
BAKER
ONETTES
PRESENTS
THING TO
ABOUT"
ws Daily
the CIRC

The Early Years

Amongst the bright lights of Los Angeles and Hollywood shines a very special star: the Bob Baker Marionette Theater. A place of wonder, magic, and memories. Opened by Bob Baker in 1963, the theater has remained a gleaming gemstone in California's crown for the last fifty-eight years.

But what is the theater's magic? The magic comes from the moment when the audience forgets reality and believes that a puppet—an inanimate object—can come to life! Jumping into your lap, giving hugs, and letting the audience be part of the show. That's magic.

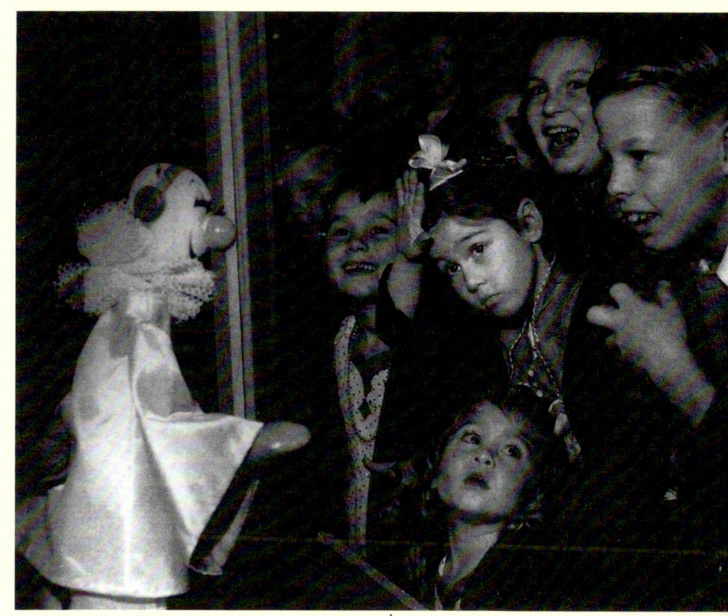

Feathers, a puppet still in use today, performs through a department store window circa 1948. Opposite: Bob Baker sits backstage among his early *Circus* Marionettes.

Puppets take many forms, from creative wax figures to the awe-inspiring mechanical pirates singing along with us on a theme park journey. In addition to established classical images of the art form—hand, rod, and marionette figures—puppets can be masks, dolls, and toys. The magic begins when the artist captures our interest and invites us into their tale.

Bob Baker often told his new puppeteers that the puppet's origins are known only to the puppets themselves. Whether they first appeared in ancient Egypt as images of the gods, or are descended from the gods themselves, as is the legend in India, is unknown. It is a fact that the puppet became part of the religious rituals of Java, Persia, China, and Japan. As civilization spread, and with it new cultures and new ideas, puppets took on added color, depth, and personality. They appeared in ancient Greece as entertainment—Archimedes, Socrates, and Plato wrote of the puppet's satiric nature and potential for social commentary.

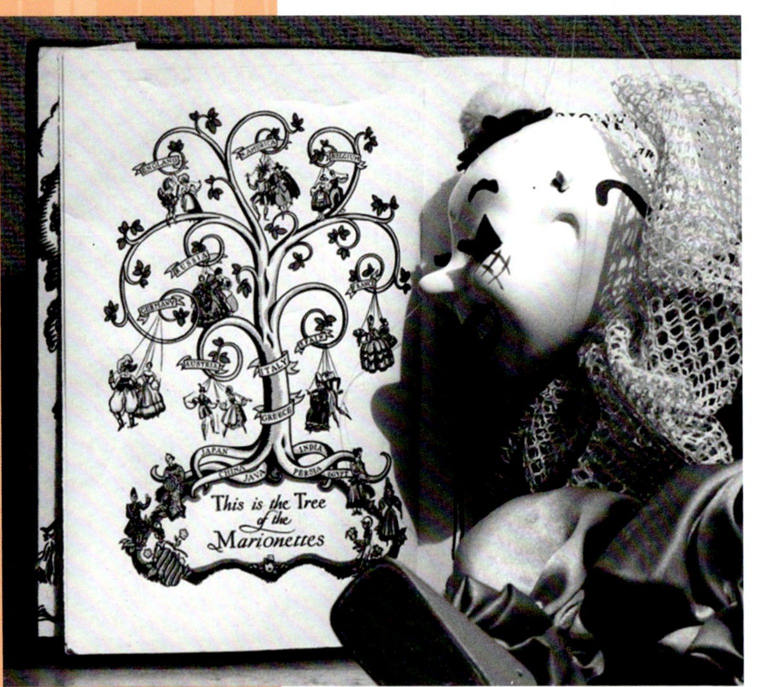

With the advent of Christianity, puppets were adopted by the church, where they were used to present morality plays. The French word *marionette* means "Little Mary," since puppets were often used to perform the nativity. From the church, the puppet became a favorite at court, and spread into cities. From there, puppets entered the theaters of Italy, France, Austria, Russia, and England. Men of arts embraced puppets: Shakespeare, Goethe, Cervantes, and Voltaire all wrote shows for puppet theaters, while Mozart and Hayden composed for them. Puppets have roots in both highbrow and popular culture, a history Bob Baker emphasized in his unique style of puppetry.

When the first European puppets were brought to America, they found their counterparts in the puppets of Indigenous Americans. Combining the ancient with the new, the puppet theater evolved into a magnificent art form. George Washington hired Punch and Judy performers for the troops. P.T. Barnum placed a puppet theater in his museum. Tad Lincoln presented puppet plays in the White House. Puppets played an outstanding role in contemporary theater, as well as in advertising, motion pictures, television, and even psychoanalysis. By the time Bob started his career, puppets—and marionettes in particular—were a popular form of entertainment, appearing everywhere from grand theaters to local department stores. Bob Baker would celebrate the art form, and take puppetry to new heights.

Robert Allison Baker III was born in 1924 to Violet Seamans Baker (known affectionately as Vi) and Robert Allison Baker Jr. (nicknamed Al). Bob lived his entire life in the family home on 219 North New Hampshire Ave. in Los Angeles.

Bob's father ran a truck and tire business, and became a top salesman for Goodyear Tire, a company that serviced Hollywood movie studios as well as a wide range of industries in Los Angeles. Bob often tagged along with his dad while servicing these businesses, giving him an inside view of the film industry and the products made by these interconnecting specialty trades, all of which influenced Bob in his future vocation.

Bobo was one of Bob's earliest and most-beloved commercial puppets; he even starred in his own TV show. Opposite: Bob Baker, at age four, sits in front of the garages that will become the home of Bob Baker Marionettes From Hollywood.

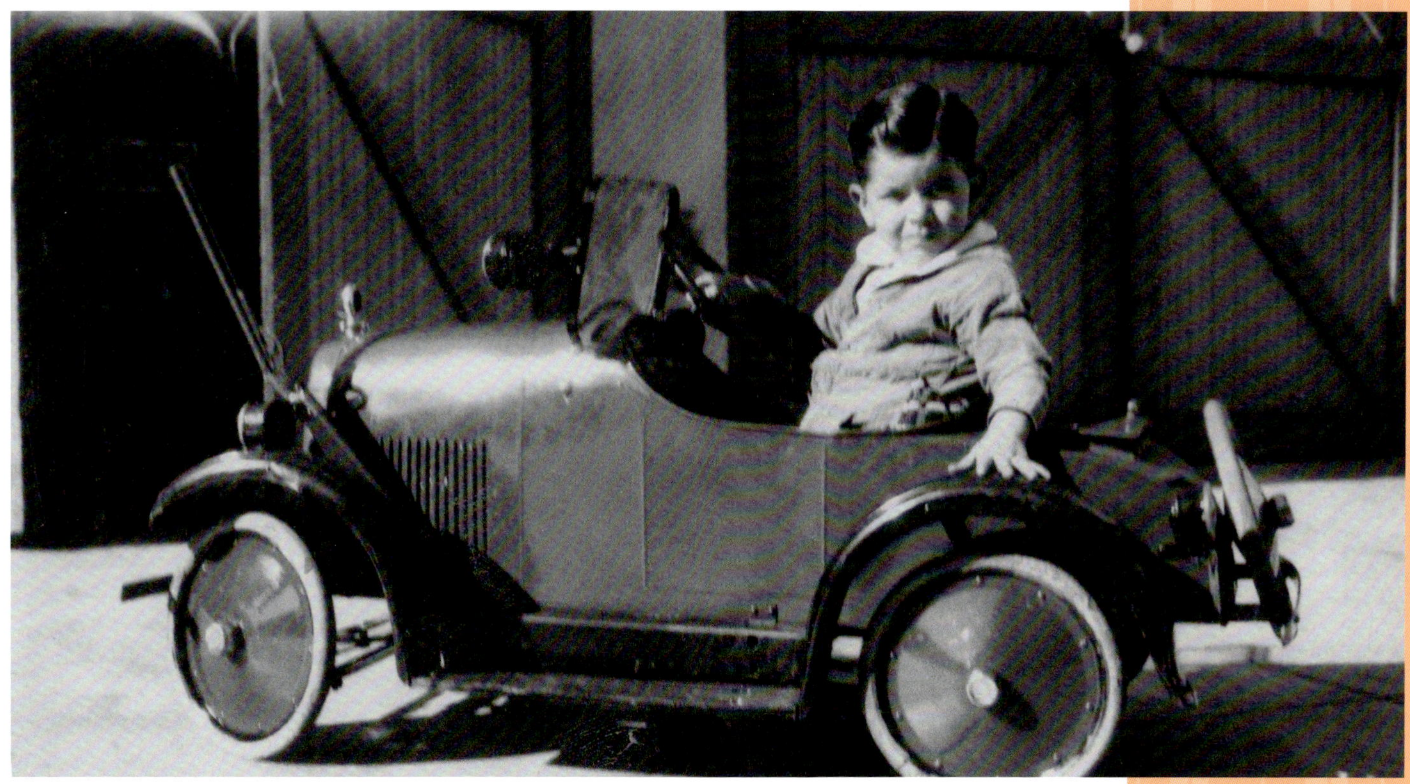

At age five, Bob saw his first puppet show at Barker Bros., a furniture and housewares store in downtown Los Angeles. Early California puppet history was greatly influenced by many of the major Los Angeles department stores. J.W. Robinson's, the May Co., Bullocks Wilshire, and others all used the art form as a way to attract consumers by featuring puppet workshops, display windows, demonstrations, and lavish full-length productions. Most of them also sold one-of-a-kind marionettes. In the 1920s, puppetry was fast becoming a fad and a fascination in America.

Although Bob could not remember the name of the performing company at Barker Bros., he vividly remembered the show. His father took him to see the early morning performance; the magic caught Bob in its spell and showed him things that forever changed his life. There was an elegant dancing ballerina, holiday toys brought to life, and one puppet in particular that caught Bob's notice: Jack Sprat, from the nursery rhyme. This specialized puppet was a "trick" puppet: on cue, the marionette could instantly become fat or thin using a balloon that formed the body of the puppet. To make Jack Sprat grow "fatter," the balloon was filled with air. To slim him down again, the air was released. However, this puppet tended to have mishaps during the show. Though the first performance went well, in the second show the balloon exploded, and in the third show it came loose and sailed into the audience. For some children, the mishap with the balloon might have destroyed the magic, but for Bob, it planted a seed. The young child was fascinated, not just by the charming performance, but by the need to know how it all *worked.* Bob realized the magic didn't just happen—it was created by a puppeteer.

Overcome by excitement, Bob knew immediately that he had found his life's passion. He

later recalled: "To heck with my electric trains; get rid of my Lincoln logs. Get rid of them. Get rid of my erector sets—I want puppets! I was six, seven, and eight, and I was an entertainer!" That afternoon, a puppeteer was born.

With his career path firmly mapped out in his mind, six-year-old Bob told his parents he should study the arts. Ever supportive of his endeavors, Bob's family enrolled him in Jack Laughlin's folk dancing class, tap dancing with Nat King, piano, German gymnastics and acting lessons with Hollywood's Max Reinhardt.

Bob was still too young to build his own marionettes, so his family bought him commercial puppets from department stores. Many famous puppeteers began their careers this way. Since the 1940s, Pelham Puppets of England have been many a young puppeteer's first experience with puppets. In Los Angeles, Bullocks Wilshire conveniently sold puppets and held demonstrations in its toy department. Bob's first puppet was a clown, followed by a Mickey Mouse puppet created by Hestwood Marionettes. (Nowadays, that puppet is the "holy grail" of Disney collectibles.) Bob's stuffed toys were soon disassembled and turned into additional marionettes. The main puppeteer for the Bullocks Wilshire store was Henriette Gordon, who was fondly called Henrie. When she saw Bob's enthusiasm for the puppets, she offered to give him private lessons. At last, Bob was taking professional puppeteering classes.

When learning an art form, there is no substitute for great mentorship. Rather than just learning abstract principles, mentorship gives a student a hands-on approach to their chosen

Bob's puppets entertain neighborhood children in his garage theater and display room. Circa 1944.

profession. When finished, the apprentice becomes the master, blending together the many different styles they were taught. And that's what happened to Bob. The Bob Baker Marionette Theater would not be what it is today without the lessons young Bob was given. His technique is made up of many different styles that influenced him. Bob had as many as twelve mentors, each one slightly altering Bob's unique style of making marionettes. And each one is important to the history and evolution of American puppetry.

Gordon began tutoring Bob in the puppet arts when he was seven years old. In addition to taking her student to the Shrine Auditorium to see the Piccoli Puppets from Italy, she sold him two Toy Soldier marionettes and supplied a phonograph record for Bob to rehearse his movements. Bob practiced two hours a day, six days a week, to the music of Leon Jessel's "Parade of the Wooden Soldiers." He would eventually wear out three records learning to march two soldiers at once in perfect rhythm, day after day. Each tap step was intricately performed to precision.

Bob was fortunate to discover his love of puppetry during the "Golden Age of Marionettes," a period when marionettes became the preferred style of puppet for almost all new puppeteers. This was because, of all the types of puppets, the marionette gave an audience the most lifelike interpretation of humanity. Hand puppets can only show part of a body, since the puppeteer's arm is usually hidden behind a stage. Shadow puppets are bound by a limited range of shapes, and rod puppets are constrained by the position of the performer—for example, if the puppeteer is positioned behind or under the puppet, the audience can only ever see the puppet within a performance space (or puppet theater) that allows limited profiles and actions. By contrast, marionettes can represent a human body from head to toe while moving around a larger area, and the strings allow for precise, subtle, and more life-like movement. Many puppeteers, who were also actors, presented live theater productions with these tiny figures. The puppets could act, dance, and sing, moving spellbound theatergoers with their

The Virgil Junior High School eighth-grade yearbook profiles Bob's newly created show *The Marionette Varieties*.

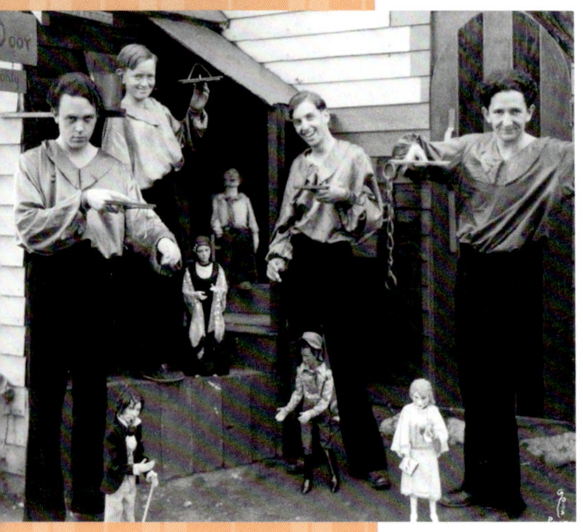

presence. Puppet shows ranged from plays, to musical revues, to vaudeville comedy, and Bob tried to see each new and exciting performance that came to Los Angeles. And with each viewing, he took away what he liked most and combined it with his own artistry.

Tony Sarg has been called the "father of modern American puppetry" because he popularized puppetry and demystified the process, making it more accessible to the general public. In 1934, Bob was lucky enough to see Tony Sarg's touring company, which was based on the East Coast, present *Faust, the Wicked Magician* at the Los Angeles Philharmonic Auditorium. Not only did Sarg create the helium balloons for the famous Macy's Thanksgiving Day Parade, his troupe also toured the States from 1919 to 1939, performing large-scale marionette shows based on classical literature. Sarg's showmanship, magic, and elaborate theatrical effects enthralled Baker and inspired him to think big.

Young Bob even examined the artistry of the European puppeteers. One of his favorites was Richard Teschner, a Viennese rod puppeteer trained in Prague. His productions were known for their whimsy and creativity, and his puppets for their expressiveness. From 1903 through the late 1940s, Teschner set a standard for art in puppetry.

The Yale Puppeteers were another favorite performing company of Bob's. Harry Burnett, Forman Brown, and Richard Brandon had opened a marionette theater on the newly refurbished Olvera Street in 1930. The theater, named Teatro Torito, featured puppet plays and songs written by Forman, with puppets constructed by Harry Burnett. Celebrities flocked to see their shows, and the trio had them sign their names in chalk on the walls of the stage. They wrote original songs for their marionettes to sing, inspiring Bob to eventually work unique song stylings into all his theater shows. When the Yale trio left to try their luck on the Broadway stages of New York in 1931, Yale puppet maker Bob Bromley and his partners, Wayne Barlow and C. Ray Smith, took over the building. By the end of 1932, Bob was regularly appearing backstage before showtime, checking marionette strings and ringing the bell for the opening curtain. He got hands-on experience learning what it takes to run a professional puppet theater, now known as the Famous Olvera Puppeteers. Many future master puppeteers began their careers pulling strings on Olvera Street.

At the time, the major department stores—Bullock's, J.W. Robinson's,

Bob's earliest influences; he derived a sense of scale from Tony Sarg (top), fantasy and whimsy from Richard Teschner (center), and original song stylings from the Yale Puppeteers (left). These influences would crystalize in his first theater, housed in one of his family's backyard garages (opposite).

TONIGHT
ONLY
The
MARIONETTE
VARITIES

and the May Co.—all had what they called "Party Shops," which were located near their toy departments and offered a one-stop, complete party service. Patrons could arrange all the entertainment and decorations through the store (a business model Bob would later adopt for his puppet theater). And that's how, in 1933, Bob got his big break at age eight. After two years of studying and helping Gordon demonstrate puppets at Bullock's, she asked him if he would like to perform at a birthday party for the child of Mervyn LeRoy, the famous Hollywood director and producer. With Gordon's help, Bob dragged his puppets, store-bought stage, and Victrola record player to the LeRoy mansion. The show was a success, and Bob received a whopping fifteen dollars for his efforts. Giddy with fame and fortune, Bob decided that, from then on, he was going to be the "puppeteer for the stars."

Word spread, and soon all the other department stores were sending Bob out to perform. With the money he made, he upgraded the Victrola to a Magnavox amplified record player and started building new puppets, scenery, and costumes. Between the ages of eight and ten, Bob began to make his own hand-crafted marionettes. Enlisting the help of a neighbor, he was soon practicing new puppet numbers and ideas on the community while also performing weekend birthday shows.

By this time, ten-year-old Bob had become a full-fledged puppeteer, and despite his young age, saw that he needed a permanent puppet theater to

Interior shots of Bob's first theater. A portable stage and director's chairs for audience members marked the early and ambitious start of his formal theatrical presentations. Bob lived on New Hampshire Avenue until his death in 2014. Throughout his life, the property would house his first theater, his studio, storage space, archives, and a multitude of puppets.

call his own. Using the limited means available to a small child, Bob transformed one of his family's four garages into his first theater. His new neighborhood puppet stage was called Bob's Petite Theater. Using store-bought marionettes and some of the first puppets he built himself, Bob would entertain relatives, curious passersby, and enthusiastic neighborhood children whenever he could. Gordon's daughter, Tina Gainsboro, helped him pull the strings as a young teen; she was Bob's first part-time "employee". Bob's artistic ambitions weren't limited by his means—he designed elaborate productions for his small home theater, at one point using so much wattage for lights that he blew out the power in his whole neighborhood.

As Bob's talents developed, his shows became more popular and in demand. His determination was unrivaled. He later recalled, "I didn't tell my dad I was *going* into the puppet business. I

Spotlight on Talent

Frank Paris

Frank Paris was one of the amazing puppeteers Bob admired when he was beginning his own career. Paris performed all over the world with his marionettes. He was a pioneer of cabaret-style puppetry, which later became a signature of the Bob Baker Marionette Theater. Paris had several successful early television shows, including *Puppet Playhouse*, the original program that became *The Howdy Doody Show*. Paris also taught puppetry at local colleges and, in his later years, built puppets for the Bob Baker Marionette Theater. Paris designed elaborate "trick" marionettes for Bob, including the theater's beloved blacklight skeletons, patterns for *Nutcracker*'s waltzing flowers, and *The Circus*'s troupe of monkeys.

was *in* it! And doing it. They either had to get me out of it, or they had to help me do anything I didn't know, and that's the way it was."

Bob admired a Broadway-style marionette show in the resort city of Avalon, on Catalina Island off the coast of Southern California. During the summers between 1933 and 1936, Bob Jones and Nick Nelson of Nickabob Puppets performed sophisticated revues for tourists waiting to get into the island casino. Their show was called the *Catalina Revue of 1934*. At age ten, Bob spent countless days traveling back and forth by boat and absorbing the lessons learned backstage with Jones and Nelson, helping work the marionettes whenever the opportunity arose. Bob networked with any puppet performers he could find. And his connection with Bob Jones was very important, because it would eventually lead to the notice of Walt Disney.

Above: A publicity still from 1937's *Artists and Models*, one of the films at the beginning of Bob's Hollywood career.

During the Great Depression, puppeteers were employed to entertain the public as part of the Works Progress Administration (WPA). The Los Angeles Puppetry Unit formed and became a part of the Federal Theater Project. Bob Bromley, Bob Baker's former mentor from Olvera Street, became the unit's director in 1936. From that year through 1939, the Theater Project, also known as the Theatre of the Magic Strings, presented such classic productions as *Captain Kidd*, *Petrushka*, *Don Quixote*, *Alice in Wonderland*, *Pinocchio*, and *Snow White*. Bob saw them all and was blown away by their production quality. He sought a position with Bromley and fudged his age to become a WPA puppeteer. When he finally came clean and admitted that he was younger than the required government age, Bromley said, "That's all right. You're not being paid. No paper trail, no problem!"

In 1937, Bob grew his talents even further when he pulled some strings in the Paramount film *Artists and Models*, starring Jack Benny. Since by that time Bob had been working with many Hollywood marionette companies, Bob Jones thought he might be a big help during the filming. Quite a few puppeteers worked on this film, manipulating Russell Patterson's art deco-designed "Pattersonettes." Joining Bob on the scaffolding were his mentors Wayne Barlow and Bob Jones, as well as the nightclub marionette performer Frank Paris.

During his last year of junior high school, Bob created new puppets for a variety-style marionette show inspired by two of his biggest influences: Paul Walton and Michael O'Rourke. The pair ran a puppet theater on Olvera Street from 1935 to 1939 called Walton & O'Rourke's Puppet Theatre, which featured fast-paced adult musical revues. The unique thing about their marionettes was that they often had fully articulated faces—moving eyes, mouths, eyebrows, and more. For his own musical revue, Bob made marionettes similar to the Walton and O'Rourke style. They included a puppet parody of the well-known comedian W.C. Fields singing and dancing, musicians performing xylophone and piano numbers, and a comedy interlude featuring a marionette ventriloquist and his smart-aleck dummy. With his new set of articulated puppets, Bob found himself getting booked for a lot more shows as the quality of his performances increased.

Around this time, Bob was contacted by vaudevillian puppeteer Mike Dietrich. Dietrich was looking for someone to build puppets for a new stage act with his partner. This would be the first time Bob would build puppets for another puppeteer. He was later hired to create more puppets for Dietrich, his partner, and the Rockettes to perform at Radio City Music Hall in the

Bob Baker marionettes, circa 1940s, depict early versions of puppets Bob would use in later shows, including a tightrope walker and marimba player.

Spotlight on Talent

René Zendejas

René Zendejas began his puppet career in 1940, when he became Bob Baker's first official apprentice while Bob was still in high school. The two men went on to become lifelong colleagues and collaborators. Appearing under the name "René and his Artists," Zendejas performed shows at Knott's Berry Farm, Universal Studios, the San Diego Zoo, Las Vegas nightclubs, as well as internationally. His work has also appeared on film and television; he designed the hit bilingual marionette television show *Domingo* for eight years. Puppets and animatronics designed and created by Zendejas can be found throughout the Bob Baker puppet collection. His Mexican hat dancer marionettes are a standout in the theater's *Fiesta*, as well as in most road shows.

production of *Toys in Technicolor*. Only this time, the puppets performed under black light, using a special paint that glows under ultraviolet light. While working for the Hollywood black-light company Shannon-Glow, Bob created black-light effects for the Ice Capades. These techniques became a signature element in all of his theater shows.

While attending Hollywood High School, Bob honed his building skills working with local teen puppeteers Jack Shafton and Bob Humes. The pair, known as the Colonial Marionettes, were a little older than Bob and went to nearby Fairfax High School. Shafton is well-known for opening the famous costume shop Shafton Inc. of Hollywood, as well as building the more than 300 marionettes needed for Sid and Marty Krofft's landmark production *Les Poupées de Paris*. Their company started in 1934, and soon were performing weekends on the pier at Venice Beach. Later, when the duo got a gig at a nightclub in San Francisco, they called themselves the Humanettes. Bob took over their road shows. From 1936 to 1937, he substituted for any of their three puppeteers at Venice Beach, and built marionettes with them whenever he could. Bob also began giving private puppet-making lessons to high school students René Zendejas and Bob Kelly. Zendejas went on to become one of Bob's most significant peers.

One of Bob's mentors, Wayne Barlow, performed marionette magic at J.W. Robinson's department store from 1934 to 1942. Barlow's puppet designs and paint finishes made a lasting impression on Bob. The theater, in the basement of the store, featured a revolving marionette stage that allowed puppets to cross from scene to scene while in motion. Bob spent many hours with Barlow whenever he could, building puppets, performing, and studying the shows. In 1941, Bob received a call saying that Barlow had fallen off the stage, and Bob was asked to perform the rest of the run for their current Disney puppet show *Dumbo*. Encouraged by his teachers, Bob was released from school and performed with the show until the production closed. Afterwards, he stayed on at J.W.

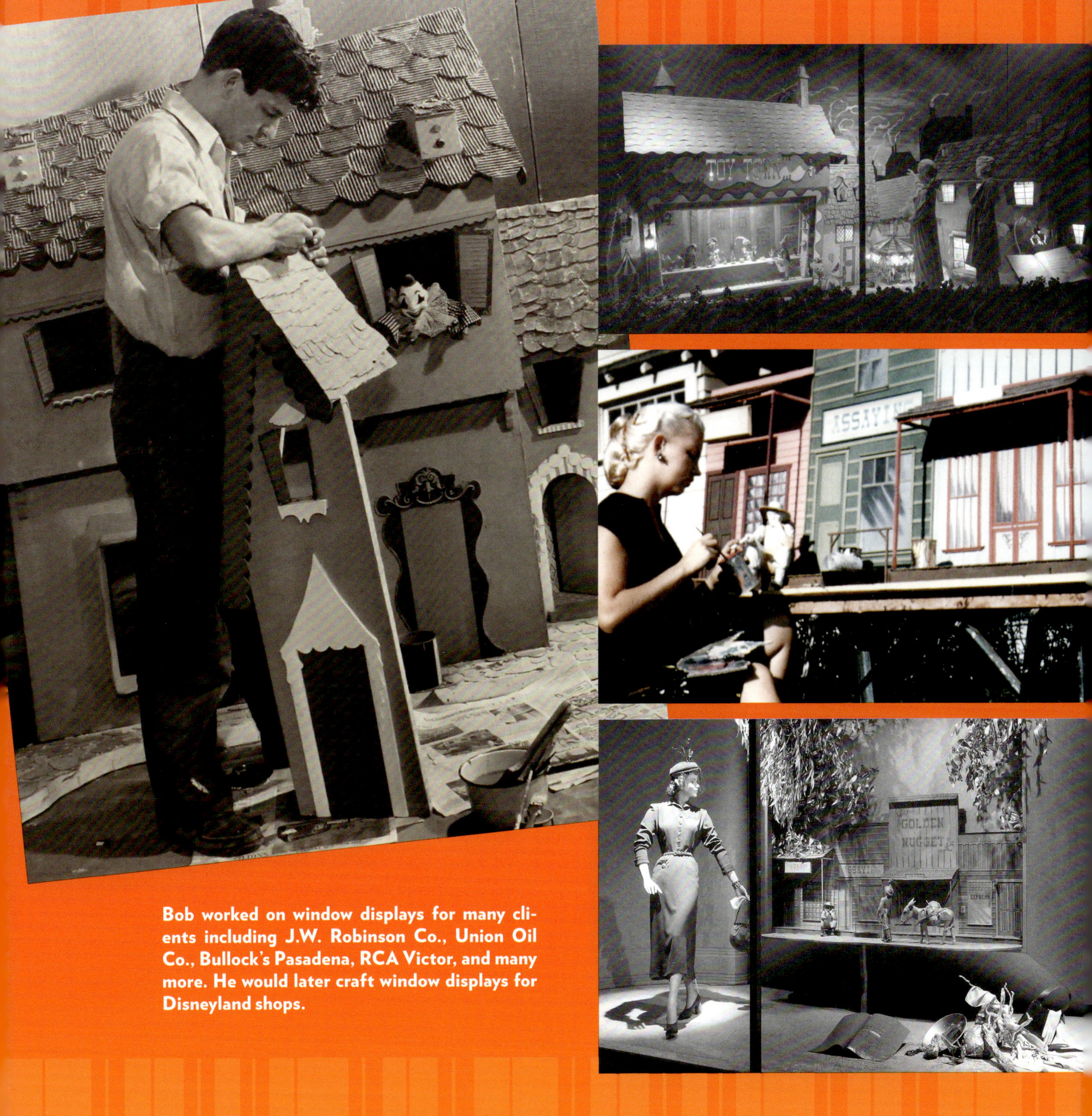

Bob worked on window displays for many clients including J.W. Robinson Co., Union Oil Co., Bullock's Pasadena, RCA Victor, and many more. He would later craft window displays for Disneyland shops.

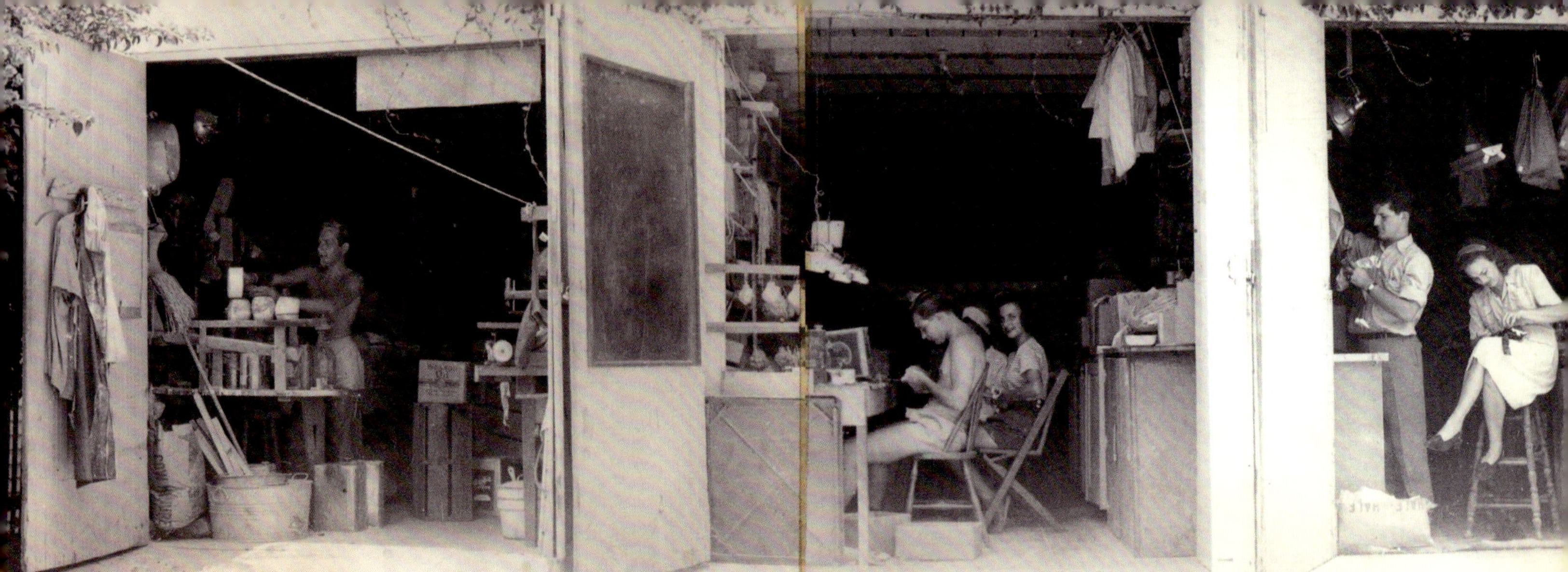

Robinson's and worked in the window display department. Despite missing time at school, Bob graduated with his senior class after making up his lost school work over the summer.

In 1941, America officially entered World War II. Bob was about to begin training with the Yale Puppeteers, who had returned to Los Angeles from New York and were preparing to open their famous Turnabout Theatre. But Bob, at seventeen, thought it was more important to enlist in the Army Air Corps. With his parents' permission, he did a brief stint as a warrant officer with the Air Corps Engineers, specializing in the 938th camouflage battalion. His main job was disguising places like the Lockheed base from enemy bombers. Many Hollywood artists were used for this type of work; huge painted canvases of endless fields could easily cover buildings that were used for military purposes, fooling enemy pilots.

Bob was released early from active duty when he became ill with a severe fever while performing his work. During his nine-month recovery period, he worked with patients using puppets as therapy to help resolve problems. He also taught puppet construction and manipulation to patients who needed help with muscle coordination. After leaving the Air Corps, Bob returned home to complete his studies at the University of California, Los Angeles, and then went on to the ArtCenter College of Design.

Bob soon found work in another puppet-related field: stop motion animation. By the end of 1942, he had begun working with renowned film director and stop motion expert George Pal. Born in Hungary, Pal had emigrated to the United States in 1939, bringing with him his style of stop motion called "replacement animation." Utilized to its fullest potential in Pal's famous *Puppetoons* short films (1940–1948), replacement animation required 9,000 individually carved and machined wooden figures or parts for a typical film. For each movement of the puppet, and for

Bob ramped up production in his backyard workshop in the mid-to-late 1940s. The successful production of more than sixteen different collectible marionettes only heightened the public's interest in Bob and his puppets.

BULLOCK'S
WILSHIRE
PUPPET PLAY
Beloved toy and teacher, the
impudent puppet . . . his family tree is
proud and many-leafed . . . the name is from the latin.
meaning doll . . . and through the ages, through the natio
men and women, boys and girls have dearly loved to play
them . . . because puppets are a constant delight, bullock's wi
has assembled a remarkable collection . . . complete with an es

every second of film, a new head or limb was used to convey motion.

Bob began working as an apprentice on the night crew, and soon found himself indispensable as a head animator. He worked on Pal's most famous *Puppetoon*, named *Tulips Shall Grow*, and on many of the *Jasper* shorts. When the threat of a union strike loomed over the studio in 1945, Bob decided to leave, rather than join, out of his great respect for Pal. But their collaboration didn't end there. Bob continued to work for Pal over the years, building items out of his own workshop—including a miniature six-inch Tom Thumb puppet for the movie *Tom Thumb* and specialized props and puppets for upcoming projects—and contributing to various Pal films as an animation advisor and animator whenever needed.

Inspired by Henrie Gordon and the marionettes he used to buy as a child, at age twenty Bob began to create his own line of specialized marionettes. From 1944 to 1950, Bob produced high-quality collectible marionettes out of his family's garages. These puppets included Cleo and Sully, a Dutch girl and boy, a girl named Suzy, a sailor, a little dog, a ballerina, and one of his most famous creations: Coco the Clown. Bob's marionettes are easily recognized by their characteristic wooden wedge feet, simple dowel controls, and flat wooden hands. Bob eventually took over all four of his family's garages, replacing his childhood Petite Theater with a casting and painting room for making heads and hands, a display area for sales, a costume and wig room, and a woodworking shop for making bodies, feet, controls, and marionette stringing.

Bob's lead costumer (top) assembles and strings each Bobo marionette (left). Thousands of the marionettes were sold to fascinated children. Opposite: Meticulous documentation of the fabrication process showed the careful handcrafted element of these masterful marionettes.

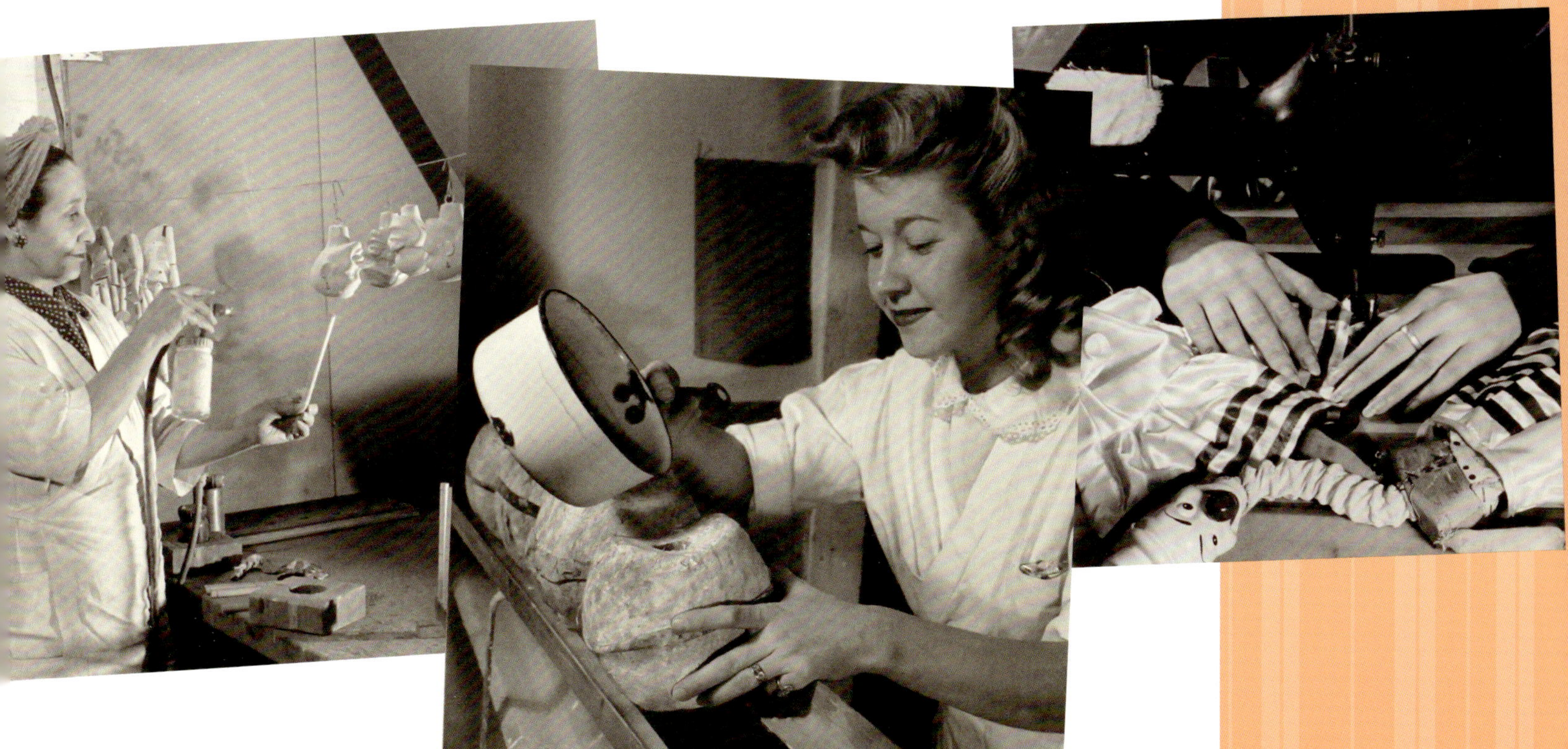

Bob named his new business the Bob Baker Marionettes from Hollywood. For his first order, Bullocks Wilshire requested 150 marionettes for Christmas sales. They ended up selling 500. By Easter, they had sold another 400. Very soon, more than fifty department stores were selling his puppets, across the nation and internationally. The prestigious list included Neiman Marcus and Saks Fifth Avenue. He quickly filled his workshop with a talented staff that included Zoe Brooke, who had worked as head painter and doll maker for Monica Dolls, known for their distinct painted features. He lured her away with a salary of one dollar an hour, when the going rate was forty cents. Brooke continued to work for Bob for many years, painting and making wigs for his theatrical marionettes and commercial puppets. At the height of production, his staff included forty artists who produced over 100,000 puppets for sale all over the world. These vintage toys are now highly sought after by collectors at public auctions and high-end antique shops. Four of the marionettes still hang in the final scene of Geppetto's workshop in the Pinocchio's Daring Journey ride at Disneyland.

By the end of 1945, Bob had outgrown the cramped family garages and moved into a small shop at 7761 Santa Monica Boulevard in Hollywood. It was in this new building, and from the previous garage workshops, that the Bob Baker Marionettes would create their shows and television and film puppets.

It was around this time that Bob and designer Morton Haack, tired of making the Coco clowns, decided to change the Coco puppet into a different type of clown, named Bobo. A new costume, a change of face paint, and Bob had instant success. Children loved Bobo, who was

named after his creator. Three wallpaper companies put Bobo on a children's line of wallpaper, and when he was added to Bob's line of salable marionettes, the pixie clown with the happy-go-lucky face outsold all the other characters three to one.

Bob had another big break in 1949: his own television show: *The Adventures of Bobo*, which aired on KFI-TV Los Angeles. The new clown was destined to star in what would be one of the first television series to originate on the West Coast. This was in the early days of television broadcasting, and so *The Adventures of Bobo* was televised from the top floor of a storage building in Hollywood. The ceilings were very low, and the puppeteers had to bend over while operating the marionettes. The show featured Bobo and many of the Baker marionettes that were currently for sale, as well as others built for various plot lines. All the fanciful sets and props were also handmade by the Baker artists. The show's music and dialogue were performed live, while the marionettes were being filmed. Actress Marion Richman supplied Bobo's voice until her untimely death, and then Bobo became voiceless.

Bobo then joined the Baker touring company as a mute puppet. He became a popular visitor at children's birthday parties, where he presented the birthday child with a very large lollipop. Bobo slowly eased into semi-retirement, appearing now and again for a specialty number or a nostalgia act in Bob Baker Marionette Theater shows.

Bob was beginning to cast quite the spell over Los Angeles, and like all great magical spells, his

Bob Baker (far left) and his partner Alton Wood pose for a publicity photo. A pragmatic foil to Bob, Alton helped realize many of Bob's elaborate and ambitious visions over the next five decades. Opposite: Bobo's appearances on *The Adventures of Bobo* made him a star.

was made up of several unique ingredients. In 1949, he discovered one very special ingredient: his future partner, Alton Wood. Bob met Alton on the television set of *The Adventures of Bobo*. Born in Mathis, Texas, Alton had spent his early years in San Antonio. An accomplished pianist, he had attended the University of San Antonio and the University of Texas, where he graduated with a B.A. in music. After studying piano in New York, Alton had moved to Los Angeles to further his music studies. But when he saw Bob Baker in performance, he was enchanted by the show's magic and gave up the piano strings for marionette strings.

Alton began working in Bob's workshop, producing puppets for sale. Soon, he mastered the art of puppet manipulation. He and Bob worked so well together that they decided to form a company—Bob Baker Marionette Productions. This grew into a successful enterprise

under Alton's financial management and Bob's creative leadership. Alton became a top performer for the company, as well as its business manager. The audience loved to watch Alton move the marionettes with his whole body in sync with his performances. It was Alton who convinced Bob to perform his marionettes "in the round," with the audience seated on the floor or sitting close to the puppets in a half circle. Alton and Bob performed with their puppets together in many movies, television shows, and commercials.

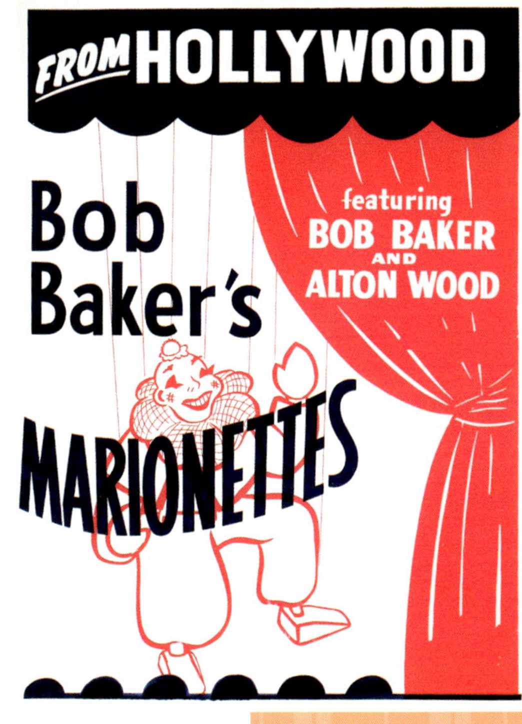

The duo's marionette shows soon became a mainstay of California county fairs. They traveled to countless schools, festivals, country clubs, and holiday gatherings—wherever they were welcomed. Their traveling road shows included *Over the Garden Wall*, a show featuring forest and garden animals as well as popular nursery rhyme characters, an annual Christmas special such as *Holiday Revue*, a magical journey of all the yearly celebrations, or *The Enchanted Toyshop*, which took viewers on a behind-the-scenes tour of a toy store with magical toys that came to life and entertained. Bob Baker Marionette Productions increased from two puppeteers to three, and eventually employed troupes of five or more. Bob and Alton were developing a personal and professional partnership that led to a lot of success, and together they began looking towards larger venues and higher-quality puppet productions.

Bob Baker and Alton Wood pose with marionettes for a promotional shot advertising their earliest marionette studio. Above right: An original screen-printed poster featuring television star Bobo.

A Recipe for Success

"The puppeteer is dependent upon a figure created of wood and cloth to depict action and feelings of emotion. To create these moods, or simulate the intricate movements of the human form, the puppeteer must have at his command many tricks of his trade, along with the art of pantomime, the use of sounds and rhythm, combined with forms of dance."

These were Bob's thoughts in a February 1964 *Valley Times* article on the opening of the Bob Baker Marionette Theater. The article referred to him several times as "Wizard Baker," who could bring puppets to life. In the article, Bob gave away one of the big secrets of a successful puppeteer: the marionette and the manipulator must be in sync with stylistic movement that's as natural as breathing, to create the image that the puppeteer has vanished and all that remains is the living puppet. But what makes a successful Bob Baker show? Skill and craftsmanship are essential, but there are other elements that make the production a treat. Music is without a doubt important. The songs and instrumentals that make up the soundtrack have to be carefully considered. Is the music engaging? Are the instrumentals suitable for the puppet theater? Does the singer's voice fit the character of the marionette? The music is the heart of the production, creating an emotional journey of various peaks and valleys alongside the puppet's interpretations of song and dance.

Opposite: An audience greets MaMa Goat during a road show presentation of *Something to Crow About*. Above: The Foot Foot Bunnies make an appearance at Laguna Arts Festival.

The various acts in the show either feature a multitude of puppets performing in a themed variety number, or they highlight a specific marionette singing a silly song or belting out a popular tune. The shows range from themed spectacles such as *The Circus* or *Fiesta*,

Spotlight on Talent

Morton Haack

Artist Morton Haack began designing puppets for Bob in early 1945, and went on to become one of his most significant collaborators. Haack has designed countless marionettes, costumes, and sets for the Bob Baker Marionette Theater; his work helped create the theater's immersive visual experience. His designs emphasize fantasy—such as in the elaborate topiaries that adorned the original courtyard—and fine detail, as can be seen in the expressive placement of the feathers on the theater's crows. Haack produced drawings and renderings for the original theater space, which also inspired the design for the new Bob Baker Marionette Theater site in Highland Park. Haack's work set a standard for the theater that lasts to this day. Beyond the theater, Haack was also a film production designer, earning three Academy Award nominations. His most notable work is the production and costume design for the first two *Planet of the Apes* movies in the late 1960s and early 1970s. He also designed the look of the famous films *Billy Rose's Jumbo* and *Please Don't Eat the Daisies*, both starring Doris Day.

to journeys and adventures like *Going Places* or *It's a Musical World*. But one thing is certain: a Bob Baker production is more of an exuberant, cabaret-style variety show than a plot-driven story.

The Bob Baker company has long practiced "theater in the round," an idea embraced by Alton Wood. When performing theater in the round, children are seated on the floor, in a half-circle configuration of no more than one to three rows. Adults sit behind them to keep an eye on the unpredictable youngsters. The company believes a marionette performance is more powerful for children if the puppets are up close and personal—at their eye level and able to be embraced. This is all made possible using cabaret-style puppetry, where the puppeteers perform in the middle of the audience, in full view. They are not hidden behind a puppet theater as with traditional puppetry, so the audience can see the puppeteers work their magic. But unlike the traditional vaudeville cabaret puppet style, Bob's puppets leave center stage and interact with the young ones—sitting on their laps, putting their arms around a child's shoulders, or even knocking the hat off an unsuspecting parent or two.

Bob began refining his unique style of puppetry at the Laguna Beach Festival of Arts and Pageant of the Masters. It was there that the style of the Bob Baker Marionette Theater truly emerged. Bob's performances at this festival became the template for other events. From 1959 to 1963, Bob dazzled Laguna audiences with huge, spectacular productions featuring up to ninety specialized marionettes.

The Laguna shows were performed once a year, yet Bob had to spend many months with

Opposite, top: Illustrated design by Blanding Sloan for *Something to Crow About*. Bob's talented team would masterfully develop these visions from concept to execution. Opposite, bottom: Finishing touches are put on both farmhouses and foliage.

designers and fabricators building the puppets and sets. Expert craftsmen Don Sahlin, Spencer King, and Ronald Martin, who specialized in woodworking and puppeteering, assisted Bob with sculpting the marionettes. Zoe Brooke handled all the facial painting and wig-making. A team of artisans sewed the impressive costumes. Hollywood production designer Morton Haack illustrated all the sets. Each marionette, which had taken up to several hundred hours to create, was valued at anywhere from $500 to $5,000, depending on which artists had created the figure, what materials were involved, and whether the puppet was used commercially or in a production.

Bob firmly believed that, as he said, "imagination is the elixir of life!" And to bring his marionettes to life, he drew from the imaginations of many talented individuals. If Bob was the conductor of the operation, his artists were the gifted musicians. Everyone

Color sketches by Morton Haack for *Something to Crow About* (1959). Puppet designs begin as doodles on paper and, once approved, are turned into larger color drawings, and eventually, full-fledged marionettes.

Ronald Martin, Bob Baker, and Alton Wood perform the opening number of *Something to Crow About*.

Alton and Bob on the set of *Something to Crow About*. The scope of this early production was enhanced by skills Bob and his team had developed during their years of commercial production, window display creation, and traveling shows. Opposite: *Crow About* was well attended from the start, an instant classic that still plays to sold-out crowds.

on Bob's team brought their own unique skills to the workshop, but they all had one thing in common: talent. When you look at the imagery of the Bob Baker Marionette Theater, you can trace the influence of these amazing artisans as it weaves seamlessly together into the signature Bob Baker style.

In 1959, Bob and Alton produced *Something to Crow About* for the Laguna Beach festival. The forty-five-minute musical show showcased morning, afternoon, and evening on Ma and Pa Goat's farm. The puppeteers presented animals and fanciful creatures, charming the audience through song and dance. Singing flowers, prancing bunnies, corncob pipe-smoking goats, an opera-singing chicken, vacationing pigs, bumbling scarecrows, waltzing willow trees, and tap-dancing frogs—these were just a few of the surprises. The puppeteers were dressed as farmers and performed under a proscenium designed to look like a barn. Bob used popular songs and clever characters to create a romanticized portrait of agricultural Americana, inspired by mid-century advertisements he had found in magazines. The craftsmanship in the production astounded Laguna audiences, from the grand proscenium down to the tiny carved carrot fingers on the vegetable marionettes. *Something to Crow About* became one of Bob's most beloved shows because it created a fully immersive environment from start to finish—every element of the show reflected its theme. This became a signature of Bob Baker shows—that the audience doesn't simply watch a performance, it experiences the world that Bob has built.

With the success of this show at fairs and festivals, Bob and Alton secured return engagements at nearly every venue where they performed. As a result, Bob began looking toward bigger and better things. His marionettes were in demand all across California as word of the fantastical shows spread. Quite frequently, the promoters of his shows failed to realize how popular they would be. Second shows were often added to accommodate the crowd, but still families would be turned away as the demand grew larger and larger.

BMB

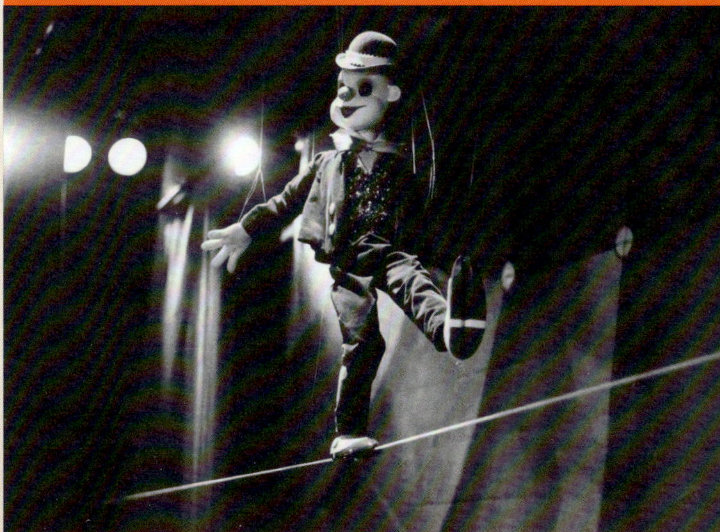

Practical effects—like using an elevated tightrope walker to shift the audience's attention upward to the top of the backdrop—characterized Bob's shows for years to come. Tricks of light, scenery, and engineering elevated the spectacle of marionette puppetry in a way that entertained and mystified audiences of all ages.

Bob had created holiday windows for Milliron's department store using a circus theme, and it had proved exceptionally popular with his audience. Bob loved the circus; the colorful visuals were perfect for attracting the eye. Since his holiday windows had been so popular, Bob decided to expand on the idea and build larger puppets for his next show at the Laguna Beach Festival of Arts in 1961.

The Circus show was a feat of imagination and engineering. The custom-made set took eight hours to assemble, and the staging weighed nearly two tons. A rotating backdrop, painted like a circus big top, opened the show, eventually revealing—in a moment of surprise for the audience—a tightrope acrobat at the top of the tent. The element of surprise became a staple of Bob's work, something that kept the audience riveted during his performances and created a sense that, in a Bob Baker show, anything could happen.

All of Bob's efforts designing *The Circus* certainly paid off; a review from *The Puppetry Journal* states, "It was well planned and typical of the wonderful work Bob Baker does; Fresh—Polished—Fast—and beautiful to see." This show soon set a precedent for other circus shows in the puppetry world. Bob's reviewers called his Laguna performance "the greatest, smallest, show on Earth!"

Captain Wilbur, the clown, and Baby Penelope, the elephant, perform one of the few live audio segments of any Bob Baker show, voiced by a puppeteer. Opposite: Musical tracks accompanied most other numbers, like this bubble bath clown (complete with a working bubble machine in the tub).

While Bob and his puppeteers toured *The Circus* throughout California fairs and festivals, his designers were already at work on their next big production. For the 1962 Laguna festival, Bob set his sights on a more elegant style of show. Morton Haack was busy working on the film *Billy Rose's Jumbo*, so Bob hired James Trittipo, a television art director and stage set designer in New York and Hollywood. Trittipo was known for not treating his set designs realistically, preferring to paint them with texture, in colors that complemented the puppets' costumes. In essence, his sets were very elegant and beautiful.

The circus theme reappeared in Bob's work for decades, as a small-scale department store production (opposite top), evolving at Laguna (above and opposite bottom).

FAT LADY
THIN MAN
MR. + MRS. TALL
THE
MADAME GULPO
SWORD
SIDE SHOW

After a fast-track work schedule, the new show, *Get Happy*, opened to rave reviews. *Get Happy* swept theatergoers away to a "happy time somewhere between today and tomorrow and a happy place, wherever that may be," as the show's host, a clown named Punchinello, announced. The spectacle began with an opening number featuring three waltzing puppeteers performing in elaborate costumes that doubled as puppet stages, performing hand-puppet versions of the French Harlequin and Columbine characters. The forty-minute production also included humorous opera numbers, a story featuring colorful witches with Dracula and Vampira, elegant waltzing couples, a breathtaking winter scene, and a French street scene with singing mice, rats, and tap-dancing cats. Another popular segment of the new show was called "Pot Au Feu." Puppeteers Bob and Alton performed numbers with "saucy" marionette vegetables that stole the show. These marionettes were originally built in 1950 for the CBS show *Veggie Fables*. Eventually finding their way into *Get Happy* years later, they also became the show-stoppers of the Bob Baker Marionette Theater production *Something to Crow About*. And at the Laguna festival, everyone was impressed.

The disparate elements in *Get Happy* could easily have made the show seem scattered or disorganized, but Bob's careful planning and attention to detail combined these characters into an elegant and entertaining variety production that was as rewarding for adults as it was fascinating to children. *Get Happy* was another leap forward in the development of a signature Bob Baker show—in which performances don't rely on story or narrative, but are bound together through the deft use of color, music, and emotion.

The cohesive concept design produced by James Trittipo for *Get Happy* united every element of the show experience from start to finish. Classical theatre, *Commedia dell'Arte*, and a harlequin motif created a one-of-a-kind visual experience.

BOB BAKER M
GET HAPPY
50¢
SHOW TIME
3:30 PM
4:30 "
5:00 "
6:00 "
8:00 "
8:45 "
9:45 "
SHOW TIME
3:00 PM
4:00 "
5:00 "
6:00 "
8:00 "
8:45 "
9:45 "

Right: Bob stands proudly in front of the real-life incarnation of James Trittipo's box office design. Above and left: Waltzing puppet stages from the opening number in *Get Happy* influenced many of Bob's contemporaries in their designs of similar walking stages.

BOX OFFICE
TICKETS 50¢
SHOW TIME
2:00 PM
4:00 "
7:15 "
8:30 "
SATURDAYS ONLY
10:45 PM

Spotlight on Talent

Bob Mason

Bob Mason originally came to Los Angeles to become a film actor, mainly in Westerns. Instead, he fell in love with puppetry, and also became well-known as a magician and ventriloquist. As a puppeteer for the Bob Baker Marionette Theater, Mason wrote comic material for puppets that was presented before the shows to warm up the audience for the main act. At the Laguna Beach Festival of Arts, Mason famously performed as a chicken who spread local city gossip. The chicken would entertain the crowd with humor and relevant stories that Mason had developed from reading that week's Laguna Beach newspaper. Mason's influence can still be seen in the comedy lines that appear in *Something to Crow About*. For five years, Mason worked alongside Alton and Bob, pulling strings at festivals, birthday shows, and the Bob Baker Marionette Theater in its first few months.

Extremely happy with *Get Happy*, the Laguna Beach festival directors asked Bob and the puppets to return with a new show in 1963. But this request came with a suggestion: Could the shows be a little more adult-friendly? Bob and Morton Haack, who had returned to the studio, pondered this and decided to create a more sophisticated revue. The result: *The Sketchbook Revue*. Bob pushed the boundaries of puppetry and placed the marionettes in more suggestive numbers, skating along the edge of nightclub puppetry, where acts are slightly more risqué.

The new Laguna show was inspired by vaudeville and inflected with camp. Musical numbers included Viennese waltzers who twirled around the stage, an American hillbilly song-and-dance team, and a very French alley scene starring a sexy black cat in diamonds and several streetwalking mice—a takeoff on a bawdy Cleopatra and her Roman escort on the Nile. In a fusion of highbrow and lowbrow cultures, the show is filled with references to nightclub culture that entertained adults and entranced children. Bob believed that his shows were never for "adults" or for "children" but rather that shows built around strong artistry and beautiful visuals would always appeal to an audience of all ages.

Although the show was considered an artistic success, the committee for the Laguna festival thought otherwise. Bob often stated that the production was "too adult for the Laguna crowd," and he was not asked back the following year. Claiming that Bob had made too many demands for the fair to oblige, the committee decided to open the selection to other Los Angeles puppet companies. Bob thought that was just fine, because he had other plans for his future.

Opposite: Many of the original puppets in Bob's shows at Laguna would later resurface in "new" shows of their own, particularly the Halloween-themed puppets like Vampira, the witches, and Dracula.

BOB BAKER
MARIONETTE
PRODUCTIONS

The wide array of puppets representing different countries and cultures were heavily influenced by Bob's extensive library of newspaper clippings, artwork, fashion magazines, and advertisements from around the world. Above: Cleopatra in her luxurious caravan, (opposite) the Accordion Mouse delights a crowd of onlookers in a moody Parisian scene.

Longtime fan favorite the Black Cat can be seen lounging in her Parisian apartment, complete with an original portrait of her donning an oversized feather hat. Opposite: Concept art for a full-fledged Parisian street scene, complete with folding scenery and dreamy backdrops.

A Palace of Puppetry

Bob's experiences at the Laguna festival taught him many things, but the most important was that his shows had found an audience. No longer content to create shows for other organizations, Bob and Alton decided in the middle of 1961 that it was time to create their own permanent puppet theater. But finding time to hunt for real estate was often difficult, since their grueling show schedule kept Bob and Alton on the road. Bob asked for help from his old friend, Tina Gainsboro, who worked with him at his Petite Theater. She found a space at 1345 West 1st Street in the Echo Park neighborhood near downtown Los Angeles. The building was big enough to house a large marionette theater, as well as several workshop areas. Built in 1953, it was a one-story structure with a simple, unassuming design and 7,500 square feet of breathing space. The building had once been a Hollywood prop shop used by Academy Award-winning scenic painter M. B. Paul; the high ceilings once used to house movie sets now facilitated a fly gallery.

Since the neighborhood was designated for urban renewal, Bob was convinced they had gotten in on the ground floor of a great opportunity. In addition, the Los Angeles Music Center was set to open in downtown in 1964, and with that, the theatrical community would come alive with a burst. Bob and Alton wanted to be a part of that burst, but their fledgling company still needed a little financial support. That support came from puppet maker Helen Crail, an older puppeteer herself who believed in Bob's dream. With her help, Alton and Bob were able to purchase the building at the end of 1961 and move their large marionette workshop. Eventually, the two men bought out Crail's share in the building and business.

Opposite: Concept art by Morton Haack for the proscenium and curtains of Bob's new theater. Above: The original party room where all sorts of celebrations were held.

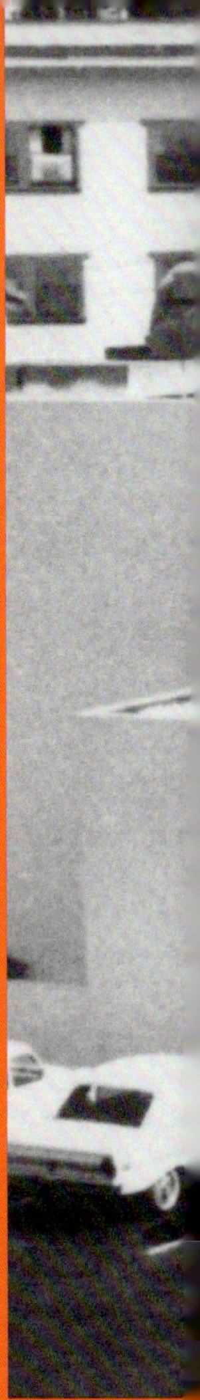

Hollywood
Fwy.
PRIVATE PARKING

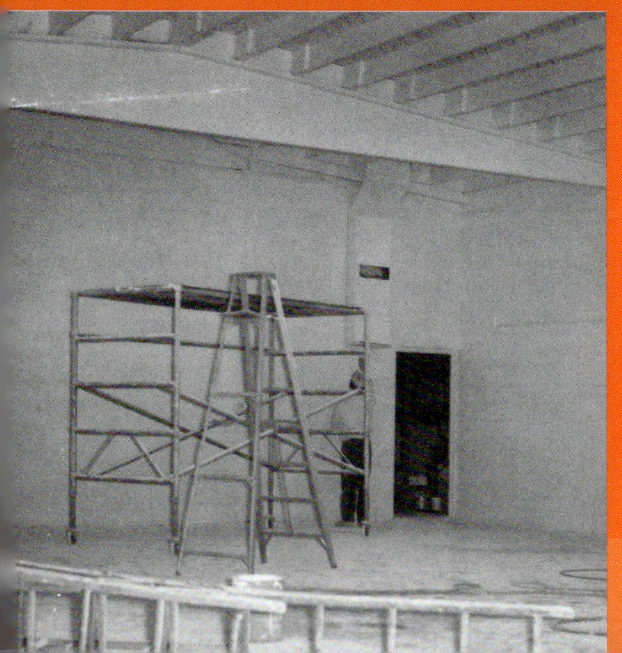

Top left: A proposed rendering of the theater facade, following a more "circus-like" vision. Left: The theater building as it looked when Bob, Alton, and Tina Gainsboro first saw it in 1961. Above: Once operations were up and running in 1963, the theater provided the perfect space for production, performance, and parties. Not pictured is the Belmont Tunnel across the street and the Beverly Bridge above the theater, placing it in a tangle of bustling surface streets, perhaps better suited for a major highway. Bob's corner theater became a drive-by landmark for commuters to and from downtown LA.

The company was anxious to open the new theater in time for the holidays, but there was a lot of work to be done. Some in the community questioned the location of the Bob Baker Marionette Theater. With the nearby Los Angeles Music Center opening its doors soon, critics wondered why they hadn't purchased closer to the theatrical heart of the city. Bob responded: "We did not want to be a part of a performing arts complex or any other institution because we wanted to be separate from human theater. We believe puppet theater is a unique art that can be practiced

Morton Haack's delicate patio, box office, and party room concepts for Bob Baker Marionette Theater feature one of the first appearances of the painted daisies on the floor—one of the theater's much-beloved recurring motifs.

effectively only in a setting where everything conforms to puppetry's need for changes in scale and proportion to fit the concept of individual puppet shows."

Bob believed that being separate, but still close, would keep the theaters as kindred spirits. Yet before construction could begin, the theater needed a design concept. While Bob was busy finishing *The Sketchbook Revue* for the Laguna Beach Festival of Arts, he and Alton hired Morton Haack and Yugoslavian art director Serge Krizman, known for his work on the original 1960s *Batman* television series, to design their new playhouse.

The final cost of remodeling the building was $125,000 ($1.1 million in 2021 dollars). But it was worth every penny. The building housed a theater and studio behind a courtyard with painted flowers, in addition to a storage space for 2,000 marionettes and props and scenery. The theater was easily identified by a huge clown named Toot perched inside the courtyard of the building, acting as a herald. Elegantly decorated in red velvet with crystal chandeliers, the theater had a grand

This early rendering of the performance space by Morton Haack is highly reflective of Bob's "nightclub puppetry" influence, stemming largely from puppeteers like Frank Paris and Bob Bromley.

NOW PLAYING
SKETCH BOOK
REVUE
FRI SAT SUN

proscenium and a beautiful party patio, where refreshments were served after each performance.The team created a remarkably beautiful theater that seated 150 patrons, with children sitting in a horseshoe on the floor and adults seated behind them on chairs.

Once the Laguna Beach contract was finished, Bob realized he had only a few weeks to open the theater before the Thanksgiving holidays. Bob hired staff for the theater, among them Tina Gainsboro, who helped bring the team together and created the family atmosphere that held the staff together through thick and thin over the years. She would make Thanksgiving dinners for the puppeteers, her own daughter amongst them.

Typical of an artist with big dreams, Bob found himself in a frenzied burst of productivity in the final hours of a project. In just three days, he and his crew spray-painted the entire building. His artists then set about decorating the various rooms, while others rehearsed and built new scenery for their opening show. Bob and his company decided to debut with *The Sketchbook Revue*. The show was well-loved by the festival crowds, and Bob had faith that the artistry and beauty of the marionettes would impress the adults, while the children would be mesmerized by the color and movement of the puppets.

The Bob Baker Marionette Theater officially opened on November 29, 1963, the day after Thanksgiving. It was a critical success, embraced enthusiastically by the public, the media, and the art world. Bob

Opposite: A crowd of eager attendees prepares to enter the theater during its first year of operation in 1963. Top right: Scenes from the always-bustling Bob Baker workshop in its first years of operation. Post-show tours for audience members gave a peek behind the scenes of puppet fabrication, and the occasional glimpse of a special project for film, television, or even Disneyland.

Spotlight on Talent

King Hall

King Hall joined the Bob Baker Marionette Theater in 1968. His techniques for building puppets with polyfoam, which made them lighter and less expensive to build, changed the way the theater built its characters. For twenty years Hall created show soundtracks, built puppets for television, and wrote dialogue and directed Bob's marionette extravaganzas. Hall also designed parade floats for Disneyland, and was the head puppeteer and designer for the St. Louis educational television show *The Letter People*. Hall acted as the master of ceremonies for the theater, and to this day his voice can be heard welcoming you to any Bob Baker production.

planned to present a variety show each year that ran from February through October, and a Christmas holiday production that opened in November and ran until the end of January.

A show at the Bob Baker Marionette Theater was a truly magical experience. After entering the daisy-painted courtyard through the ornate metal gates, visitors were transported into the world of puppets. The puppets performed on the floor, with the puppeteers parading the figures around the audience. Royal red carpets and curtains framed the stage opening, which was highlighted by three gorgeous antique chandeliers. Fantastic sets and lighting effects created a fantasy environment from a mix of sophisticated and humble materials— the lights were fashioned out of used coffee cans he had on hand. After the show, everyone came backstage into the workshop to see how the puppets were made. To end the day, families were seated in a fantasy-filled party room where coffee, punch, and ice cream were served.

Bob's workshop, which was in a constant flurry of creation, was his pride and joy; he had equipment and materials he could have only dreamed of as a young puppet maker. Besides the theater shows, the Bob Baker Marionettes continued to perform on the road at fairs and festivals, as well as appearing in films, on television, and even in commercials. Although he rarely built the puppets himself, Bob handled all

Opposite, top: Tina Gainsboro has worn many hats at the theater, from spotlight operator, to real estate hunter, and much more. As is common at a small theater, everyone did a little bit of everything. Above: Bob Baker and Sandi Price are joined by the Money Cats to break in the new stage at 1345 W. 1st St.

sculpting duties and painted all the completed parts. Yet he still found time to oversee his workshop, the theater and its professional contracts, and to perform in road shows.

The theater also housed an extensive library that included Bob's vast collection of books, magazines, and recordings that he used for reference and inspiration. Drawings and concept art for puppets, set designs, and audiovisual material were all kept within easy reach. This was the only place in the theater under lock and key, inaccessible even to staff. Bob never

Above, left to right: Ronald Martin, Bob Baker, Sandi Price, Alton Wood, and Roy Raymond dressed to the nines for a waltz with their elegant puppet partners. Left: The stage is crafted for a child's sightline. Opposite: Ron Martin and Bob Baker, each with a pair of ragdolls, welcome everyone to *All Aboard for Gingerbread Square*.

Nutcracker toy parade marches across the Bob Baker Marionette Theater stage.

locked his cash box, but his library was a private space for creation, and the theater staff revered it as the physical manifestation of his powerful imagination.

Bob and Alton were thrilled with their new theater, but one expected element never came to fruition; the neighborhood had been slated for urban renewal, which never came to pass. The bustling crowds and new businesses that were expected never arrived, and there was minimal foot traffic around the theater. During the first weeks of shows there were sometimes only a handful of people in the audience. Many of the puppeteers felt that they should cancel some of the performances. But Bob was insistent that the show should go on and the performances should be as spectacular as ever, regardless of how many patrons were there. And one day, a member of the audience was so charmed by the marionettes that she approached Bob and offered to pay the ticket price for a year's worth of unsold seats.

From 1963 through 1979, the theater's performance schedule included shows as well as past hits like *Enchanted Toyshop*, *Over the Garden Wall*, *The Circus*, *Get Happy*, *The Sketchbook Revue*, and, of course, *Something to Crow About*. Bob firmly believed that these fantasies and revues created memories for children that would be cherished their entire lives. He later recalled: "When you go to the theater, you pay admission and watch a show, with nothing but a piece of paper in your hand. But you take home the illusion, the fantasy, the love, the drama, the music, and you'll always have it."

Opposite: *Fiesta*'s giant Rhea Bird and Tango Dancers are just a part of the theater's celebration of Central and South America. Top right: The quintessential Bob Baker party hosts—Birthday Dogs Happy, Aloysius, and Percy. Bottom Right: Umbrellas, hanging swirls, Japanese lanterns, and clown table pieces are all part of the decor for the party room at the theater. 1964.

The Bob Baker Marionette Theater's most beloved show of all opened in 1973. The Bob Baker version of *Nutcracker* is an offbeat, quirky retelling of the Tchaikovsky ballet. Bob eschewed the traditional narrative and instead produced a spectacular revue that highlighted the motifs of the ballet while giving himself the freedom to experiment with dancing flowers, berries, and ice-skating gumdrops. Tchaikovsky's orchestra was replaced by Spike Jones's trumpets and whistles. Six years of work were required by over fifteen artists and craftspeople to produce over 120 different puppets for the show. In addition to marionettes, the show featured rod puppets, shadow puppets, and hand puppets. "In trying to create this

Left and opposite: Concept art for *Nutcracker*'s puppets. Above and opposite, from left to right: The Nutcracker Prince, Fairy Godmother, Nutcracker, and Mouse King appear in front of a scenic drop from the show. These marionettes were much larger and more maneuverable than their hand-puppet counterparts pictured below on the opposite page.

Hand puppets of characters from Bob's *Nutcracker* show. In the revived production of this show, all of the characters have been refashioned as marionettes.

Nutcracker was very specifically designed for the parameters of Bob's theater—four-foot tall flower waltzers took advantage of the open stage while line-ups of intricate and nearly identical puppets (and their puppeteers!) created a full and dynamic stage show.

Spotlight on Talent

John Leland

When Morton Haack moved on from the theater, John Leland became the main designer for the Bob Baker Marionettes. For close to sixty years, Leland and Bob combined their talents to create lavish presentations and costumes, and worked closely together on projects for film and television, Disneyland, and Disney World. When not working at the theater, Leland was also the display manager for The Broadway, a large department store known throughout the city. Many of Leland's elaborate painted backdrops are still in use, as is his charming and whimsical painting on the puppets' faces and clothing.

masterpiece, we had to take certain creative liberties to fit into the requirements of our troupe," Alton explained to the press.

In 1981, Los Angeles celebrated its bicentennial, and Bob wanted to create a show to honor the occasion. *LA Olé!* featured a delightful, and often humorous, look at Los Angeles and the history of this multicultural mecca. Designed by John Leland, King Hall, and other Bob Baker artists, the show demonstrated what made the City of Angels so special. Each new number was introduced by a newspaper headline that announced what the audience was about to see. Starting with a young Mexican boy and his burro sharing the tale of the beginnings of Olvera Street, the show moves on to present a song-and-dance number about the discovery of oil that features a dinosaur tumbling into La Brea Tar Pits and a dancing oil rig kickline. Toy teddy bears in racing cars try to explain the Los Angeles freeway system. Earthquakes play their part—disco dancers gyrate to "L.A. Shake," a number about awaiting "the big one." And as a finale, the marionette children of Los Angeles sing about their shared dream. Bob called it a show 200 years in the making!

LA Olé! was the last major show that Bob designed from scratch. He preferred to focus his energy on building new puppets and adding new numbers to existing programs. And by this time, most of his team of artists had moved on to other jobs, making it hard to create new shows while running the theater full-time. Building puppets was always Bob's passion—he loved to design new characters and creations. The staff always joked that Bob only ran the theater to support his puppet-making habit.

Opposite: A hand puppet named King Carlos, a blacklight homage to La Brea Tar Pits, an oil rig kickline, and "Hollywood Mice", who long for their place in the spotlight, were all part of the action in *LA Olé!*.

HAPPY BIRTHDAY
LOS ANGELES
1781 — 1981

BOB BAKER
MARIONETTE
THEATER
PRESENTS
L.A. Olé!

A raucous skating sequence from *LA Olé!*, celebrating LA's 200th birthday. Author Randal Metz stands just under the proscenium holding a clown in a yellow coat from the popular show's 1986 revival.

Though the theater gave Bob's shows a permanent home, he continued to perform throughout Southern California at festivals, private events, and community gatherings—all while expanding his troupe of puppets and puppeteers. Pictured here are veteran puppeteers Tom Ray (left, in orange) and Greg Williams (top right, pictured with Bob Baker).

BOB BAKER
NEXT

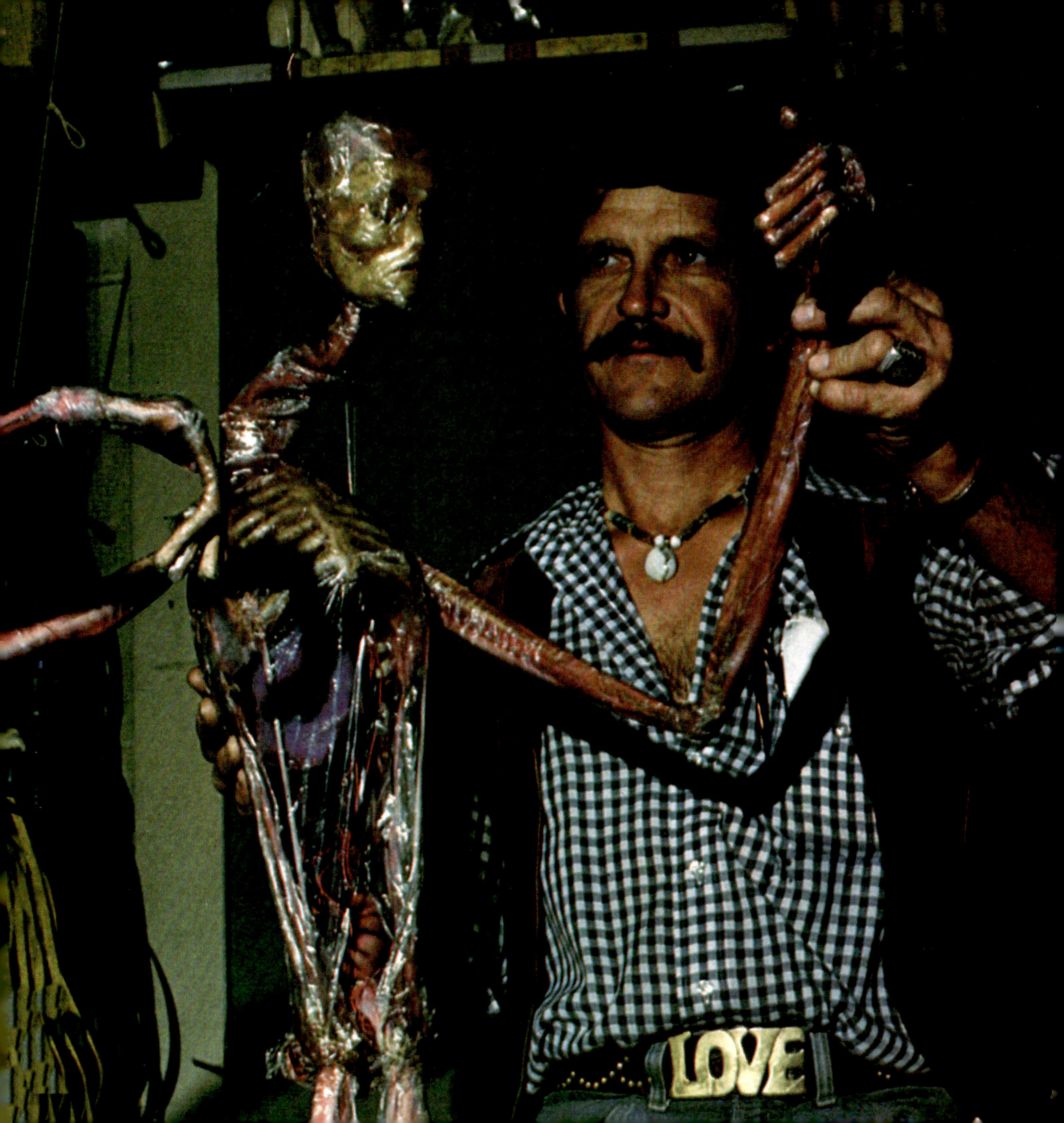
LOVE

Hooray for Hollywood

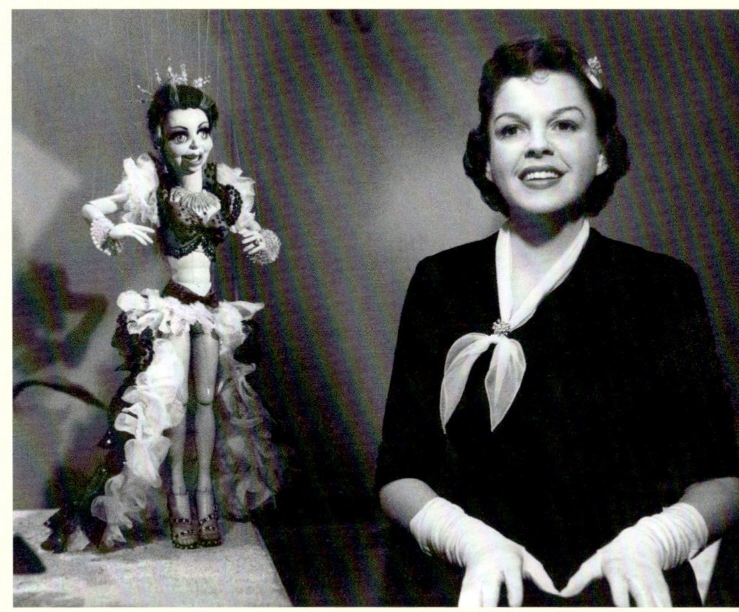

Since he grew up in Los Angeles, it was only natural that Bob would develop a great love and respect for the film industry. As a young man, he performed at the birthdays and holiday celebrations of many celebrities. From parties for Doris Day and Debbie Reynolds, to celebrations for Mervyn LeRoy and Ronald Reagan, Bob made a name for himself among the industry's movers and shakers—so it didn't take long for his marionettes to move from Hollywood homes to Hollywood movies.

One of Bob's earliest projects working in films was at the age of eight, helping his mentors Harry Burnett and Forman Brown, of the Yale Puppeteers, manipulate the many marionettes needed for the 1933 film *I Am Suzanne!*, starring Lilian Harvey. Three years later, he helped move ice-skating puppets in Shirley Temple's *Poor Little Rich Girl*. Soon Bob found himself on the backlot often, lending a hand whenever a puppeteer was needed.

Bob was often contracted to design marionettes for use in films, such as *Close Encounters of the Third Kind* in 1977 (opposite) and the 1954 remake of *A Star is Born* starring Judy Garland (above).

By 1942, he was building puppets for films and receiving full credit for his work. His first big break was in 1944, when he designed the puppets for the famous Edgar G. Ulmer classic *Bluebeard*, starring John Carradine. After this film's success, Bob's talents and skills were suggested whenever a puppet was needed in a film. As television started to take hold, puppets began to migrate toward the smaller screen, and Bob was soon working there as well. His first television projects were in 1949, with *The Adventures of Bobo* and *Moppet and Mr. Scherzo* for KFI-TV Los Angeles and Channel 5. In the late 1960s, he tried making his own short films featuring his marionettes. *Family Picnic* was a twelve-minute short film using

Spotlight on Talent

Roy Raymond Etherington

In 1960, after being trained to make puppets for the famous Cole Marionettes of Illinois, Roy Raymond Etherington traveled to Los Angeles and took up residence in the workshop of the Bob Baker Marionette Theater. For thirty years, he entertained families at the theater with his fine marionette manipulation. Etherington voiced a variety of marionettes, such as Demi Star, Pierre the Rabbit, and Happy the Birthday Dog. For close to twenty-five years, Etherington was the official guide for the puppet workshop tours at the end of each performance. He also performed with Bob in the classic films *Close Encounters of the Third Kind* and *Bedknobs and Broomsticks*, and the television shows *Bewitched* and *Voyage to the Bottom of the Sea*.

puppets that Bob and Alton created for other shows. This feature was about a family of bunnies who learn important family values while trying to enjoy their day. Bob always hoped one day to produce puppet shorts for movie theaters.

The Bob Baker Marionette Theater built exclusive puppets for films, supplied puppeteers and actors, designed props and sets, performed stop motion puppetry, and even handled specific or costly special effects for movie masterpieces. This was all before the use of digital technology and other modern filming miracles. Sometimes the movie directors took his expertise in a different direction. Bob loved to tell the story of working with director Roger Corman. For *Monster from the Ocean Floor*, Bob was hired to create a puppet sea monster that could be used for Corman's underwater shots. Bob worked long hours on a monster that could be easily filmed. To create the illusion of being underwater, he carefully glued hundreds of single barbules, or fringes, onto the puppet from the plume of an ostrich feather. When filmed with a filter, this gave the feeling of underwater movement when the individual feathers undulated with the puppeteer's manipulation. Corman thought the puppet was great—until he submerged the figure in a tank of water, which of course caused the feathers to cling limply to the puppet and not move at all. "But shouldn't it have looked like it's wet?" Corman asked Bob, who replied, "Things underwater don't look wet."

Bob and his puppeteers also filmed hundreds of commercials for television. Clients included liquor and cigarette companies, automobile manufacturers, banks, detergent makers, and food companies. For MD Tissue, Bob made the famous MD Tissue Twins puppets. One time he was asked to turn a bar of soap into a marionette. Using four invisible strings and two puppeteers, the soap was filmed as it magically scrubbed up and down a bather in the shower all by itself.

The Bob Baker marionettes have performed on numerous television series. Bob's team built puppets for the bilingual educational show *Villa Alegre*,

and created and performed all the puppet creatures for the ABC-TV Saturday morning children's show *Curiosity Shop*, developed by George Pal.

The Famous People Players is a black light theater company founded by Diane Dupuy in Toronto. The company employs young people who suffer from physical and intellectual disabilities. Dupuy trains them to be puppeteers who manipulate large props and celebrity figures using the black light technique as a way of masking the performer from the audience. One of the many benefactors of the company was Liberace, who invited the players to perform with him in Las Vegas. But Liberace said he felt that their large celebrity puppet caricatures, which the players had built themselves, needed some pizzazz. Since Bob had made puppets for the 1952 television hit *The Liberace Show*, Liberace suggested that Dupuy have the Baker company design large-style celebrity heads with articulated faces for her puppeteers to perform under black light. Liberace even paid Bob to make the first set of celebrity heads. During the fifteen-year span that Bob worked with them, he designed over sixteen animated celebrity heads. Figures included Stevie Wonder, Anne Murray, Willie Nelson, Michael Jackson, Mick Jagger, Liza Minnelli, and a host of others. Bob's puppets can be seen in the 1984 television movie *Special People,* starring Brooke Adams.

As a sideline business, the theater also manufactured costumes for promotional characters. Two popular icons from the 1980s that Bob helped promote were the popular piano-playing moon character Mac Tonight for McDonald's, and McGruff the Crime Dog, who "took a bite out of crime!" Both were featured in television commercials. For McDonald's, Bob created huge plastic, vacuum-formed heads for Mac Tonight's promotional appearances. The heads were produced in the hundreds, painted and supplied with custom props, and then sent to actors, who made

Alongside some of the more high-profile films Bob worked on were smaller productions, including the ABC show *Curiosity Shop* produced by Chuck Jones (above, left and center), and Liberace and the Famous People Players (right).

personal appearances in McDonald's restaurants across America. For the National Crime Prevention Council, the theater mass-produced fur-covered heads and hands for McGruff the Crime Dog, to be used by actors who appeared at schools and special events to help promote crime awareness and personal safety. The rest of the characters' costumes were supplied by the promotional companies.

Bob was also active in Hollywood unions. When Bob started working in Hollywood, puppeteers were not fairly compensated for their talents. In the early 1940s, if a puppeteer wasn't seen on film, the Screen Actors Guild suggested they join IATSE—the International Alliance of Theatrical and Stage Employees. This union represented prop builders and special effects artisans. However this union didn't include puppeteers. By the late 1950s, Bob thought that puppeteers working in film were treated very shabbily. One afternoon, after performing for Ronald Reagan's son at his birthday party, Bob began discussions with Reagan who was then president of the Screen Actors Guild. Reagan agreed that since puppeteers took direction from the director, they should be considered actors. And so puppeteers became part of the Screen Actors Guild. By the time Bob's company filmed *G.I. Blues*, he was considered a principal performer and had his own dressing room.

By the late 1970s, puppeteers realized Bob's initial negotiations, which SAG was still operating under, were out of date. Tony Urbano, one of Bob's earliest apprentices, along with Eren Ozker and others, responded by forming the SAG Puppeteers Caucus to advocate for puppeteer's rights. Thanks to Bob and Tony, future puppeteers working in film, television, or commercials, regardless of their involvement, are considered Principal Performers and enjoy residuals for their contributions. Bob went on to become a member of AMPAS, the Academy of Motion Picture Arts and Sciences, as well as for the Television Academy of Arts and Sciences where he served as a Governor in the animation branch.

As filmmaking technologies slowly changed from physical to digital, Bob performed less and less on camera. The 1980s and 1990s marked the beginning of the end of live-action puppets on set. As Bob was busy running a full-time puppet theater, he needed to focus his time elsewhere. In subsequent years, the Bob Baker Marionette Theater has continued work in film and television—there has been a resurgence of interest in practical effects and puppetry, and Bob Baker artists have contributed their skills to various projects. The theater has made puppets for music videos, television shows including *What We Do in the Shadows*, and more.

Above: Bob Baker fabricated the head for the "Mac Tonight" character used by McDonald's in the late 1980s. Opposite: Bob consults with director Mel Epstein about a specific shot in the 1947 featurette *Paris in the Spring* as puppeteers wait on the bridge. 1947

LEO

Here are some of the Bob Baker puppets that have appeared on film and television:

▲ *Paris in the Spring*

1947 • Also known under the title *Curtain Time*, this comedy featured lead actors Roger Dann and Sally Rawlinson, as well as Bob Baker. The plot: Dann's character is in love with Rawlinson's character, the daughter of a puppeteer, but is thwarted because he is not a success. This feel-good, romantic short featurette ran as a companion film at movie theaters and highlighted some of the best numbers and marionettes produced by the Bob Baker Marionette Theater.

▶ *Hunt the Man Down*

1950 • In this thrilling film noir picture directed by George Archainbaud, the Bob Baker Marionettes are seen performing in a small segment of the film. Gig Young portrays a public defender who dedicates himself to defending a destitute man accused of murder in a twelve-year-old trial case. To do so, he has to track down witnesses from the earlier trial. One of them is an assistant puppeteer at the Show Box Theater. Bob's circus puppets, as well as many unfinished marionettes, are featured in a confrontation scene at the theater.

◀ *The Liberace Show*

1952–1969 • Bob's company was given the job of building puppets for a commercial spot advertising the banking industry on Liberace's variety show. For this ad, he designed marionette versions of Liberace's brother, George, and his wife, Jayne. Since Bob had worked on other projects with Liberace, he was perfect for the task. For this minute-long ad, Bob made miniature versions of the couple and recreated the set and shadowed orchestra they performed with on the show. The marionettes were fully animated, with moving eyes and mouths.

Spotlight on Talent

Don Sahlin

Puppet master extraordinaire Don Sahlin first began building commercial puppets with Bob in his teens. They went on to work together in films and for George Pal Productions, animating and creating stop motion puppets. Sahlin was responsible for most of the fine craftsmanship on Bob's marionettes for the Laguna Beach Festival of Arts. He built puppets for the original *Howdy Doody Show*, created duplicate figures for Burr Tillstrom's *Kukla, Fran and Ollie*, and was the main animator for Michael Myerburg's stop motion film *Hansel and Gretel*. He is most remembered for designing the unique look of Jim Henson's Muppets. Sahlin built all of the original Muppets, as well as the Muppet characters for *Sesame Street*.

▶ A Star Is Born

1954 • One of Judy Garland's most famous movies originally featured a song-and-dance number by Judy and the Bob Baker marionettes. Garland's character's first professional job is singing a song for a commercial, performed by Bob's marionette "Taquita." The black-and-white sequence was ultimately edited out of the film. When the movie was restored in 1983 and re-released in theaters, the puppet number was edited back in, as well as several missing sections.

▲ G.I. Blues

1960 • Elvis Presley plays a soldier who tries to impress a woman at a puppet show in Europe. When the show has problems, in order not to disappoint the children, Elvis sings with the puppet characters. These puppets had animated faces and were designed by Morton Haack. Bob often told a story about how Elvis had to stop the filming and go to his dressing room to compose himself, because the puppet was so realistic. He yelled, "I can't sing to this thing!" when he realized that he was being upstaged by a doll.

Hawaiian Eye

1959–1963 • Set against the tropical beauty of Honolulu, this series centers around the cases of a Hawaiian private eye team. Connie Stevens plays Cricket Blake, a madcap nightclub singer and photographer who joins the team. In season 2, episode 10, "Girl on a String," Cricket acts as an assistant to a puppeteer who is under investigation for murder. Eagle-eyed Bob Baker fans will notice that the puppet of Stevens is actually the same marionette used to portray Jayne Liberace in the 1955 *Liberace Show* commercial.

Snow White and the Three Stooges

1961 • The Three Stooges—Larry, Moe, and Curly—take the place of the seven dwarfs in this silly musical retelling of the Snow White tale that features puppetry and ice skating. Five-time world figure-skating champion Carol Heiss plays Snow White, to Edson Stroll's Prince Charming. Directed by Walter Lang, the movie is more child-friendly, as it goes beyond the Stooges's slapstick routines. The puppet created by the Bob Baker Marionette Theater was designed by Morton Haack.

◀ Star Trek

1966–1968 • Gene Roddenberry changed the future of science fiction fantasy with his *Star Trek* television show, and Bob was there to bring an unusual character to life. In season 1, episode 1, titled "The Man Trap," lieutenant Hikaru Sulu cares for a carnivorous plant named Beauregard. That plant was actually a glove puppet created and performed by Bob Baker. Officially called a Beauregard Weeper from the planet Zeta Reticuli, the plant undulates and sways when it is attracting prey, giving off a chiming, melodic hum like a harmonium.

▼ Bewitched

1964–1972 • In season eight, episode eight, "TV or Not TV," Samantha's daughter, Tabitha, becomes a TV star when she enchants herself into a children's show to reprimand the puppets Punch and Judy. She tries to teach them to be kind and not to hit one another. Bob not only made the puppets, he and his puppeteers were also actors in the episode. Roy Raymond played Punch, while Bob did the vocals for Judy.

Bedknobs and Broomsticks

1971 • **This delightful live-action and animated film stars Angela Lansbury and David Tomlinson, and tells the story of three children who meet an apprentice witch who is learning magic to help the war effort and defeat the Nazis. Bob was hired as a technical consultant, and created all of the clothing and suits of armor that were brought to life by the magic of Angela Lansbury. He also helped to marionette Angela Lansbury on her broom by flying her broomstick on two strings when she appeared to crash into a tree. In reality, they flew her out of the tree, and then ran the film backwards to look like she crashed.**

In addition to providing the props and puppetry for scenes in the movie, including the dancing clothing for the "Substitutiary Locomotion" sequence, Bob Baker and his team created elaborate window displays for the Emporium at Disney World that recreated the animated undersea scene.

◀ Shanks

1974 • This horror film is about a deaf and mute puppeteer who manipulates the dead like his puppets. This is the last movie that shock director William Castle produced, and was the first major film to feature the renowned French mime Marcel Marceau. Bob's company built and manipulated all of the marionettes featured in the film. Marceau, who choreographed the movements of the actors, also insisted that he be trained by Bob himself to work the marionettes during filming.

▼ Escape to Witch Mountain

1975 • This fantasy and science fiction film from Walt Disney Productions centers around a sister and brother, played by Kim Richards and Ike Eisenmann, who discover they are extraterrestrial children trying to reunite with their own kind on Earth. The Bob Baker marionettes are manipulated in a scene where the children bring their toys to life. The theater's rag dolls from *The Enchanted Toyshop*, as well as the Dodo Birds from *Something to Crow About*, steal the scene. Ray Milland and Eddie Albert also co-star.

▶ Close Encounters of the Third Kind

1977 • This landmark film by Steven Spielberg starred Richard Dreyfuss as a man whose life changes after encountering an Unidentified Flying Object. The Bob Baker marionettes were tasked with the job of bringing the aliens to life in the final scenes. Bob built the six-foot-tall figure that made the first alien appearance out of the ship. The puppet "breathed" and featured internal body lighting. Spielberg originally cut Bob's puppet from the film, but then reinstated it, since it moved so elegantly in the fog-filled environment. A Carlo Rambaldi "alien" with mechanical facial features and movements was used for the close-ups, while Bob's was used for the longer shots featuring the alien ship.

Disney on Strings

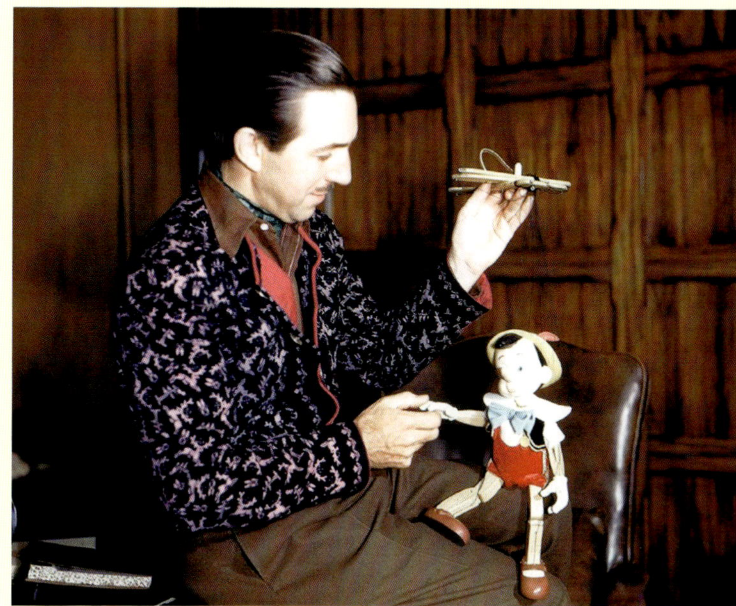

Walt Disney with a custom-made Pinocchio marionette. Opposite: Bob holds his "Sorcerer Mickey" and "Steamboat Willie" marionettes produced for commercial sale for the Walt Disney Company.

Bob Baker has been described as Walt Disney's modern-day Geppetto. Bob always had a love for all things Disney, and his childhood was influenced by the rise of Mickey Mouse's stardom. At age eight, Bob bought his first Disney puppet, Mickey Mouse, designed by Harold and Robert Hestwood. The Hestwoods were two brothers trained in the puppet arts by the famous American puppeteer Tony Sarg. When they left his troupe in the early 1930s, the brothers started presenting Mickey Mouse cartoon puppet shows at the Bullocks Wilshire department store. Around 1932, the store asked them to create a marionette line of puppets based on the Mickey Mouse cartoon classics. This was the first time Disney characters were licensed in puppet form, and the popular Hestwood shows helped boost sales.

In 1933, eight-year-old Bob wrote to Walt Disney at his Hyperion Avenue studio and asked if he could "look around." He received a polite note from Disney's secretary explaining that, with so many cartoon characters running loose all over the place, they could not allow a little boy to visit on his own. And it wouldn't be fair to all the other little boys and girls who also wanted to do so, but couldn't. This did not discourage Bob, who was determined to one day work at that magical place.

In 1937, thirteen-year-old Bob was working with Wayne Barlow and Bob Bromley at the J.W. Robinson's department store in downtown Los Angeles, adding last minute finishing touches to their production of *Snow White and the Seven Dwarfs*. The department store show

January 19, 1934

Master Bobby Baker
Goodyear Service, Incorporated
1415 East Ninth Street
Los Angeles, California

Dear Bobby:

It is a strange thing, isn't it, Bobby, that mothers know about almost everything? All the artists, musicians, and story-writers at our studio are very busy indeed. Mickey and Minnie, and the Three Little Pigs, and Pluto are dashing up stairs and down, singing songs, dancing, and what not.

You see, we cannot allow one little boy to come to visit our studio, because that would not be fair to all the other little boys and girls who want to come. We are sure you understand.

You seem to have forgotten to send along your business card. We hope this does reach you, because we want to tell you that we are happy to know how fond you are of Mickey Mouse and the Three Little Pigs.

Yours very sincerely,

WALT DISNEY PRODUCTIONS, Ltd.

By Dolores Voght
Dolores Voght
Secretary to Mr. Walt Disney

DV FJO
Enclosure 1

SILLY SYMPHONY
Sound Cartoons

was set to open in advance of the movie's premiere, with marionettes crafted in the likeness of Disney's designs and sound recordings of the original movie soundtrack, all furnished by the Disney studio. Walt Disney himself came to see the final product, and was very impressed with the promotional show. It was at this show that Bob met the man he so admired. He was in heaven.

After that, Bob soon found himself on a personal tour of Walt Disney Studios. Bob Jones, who had mentored Bob at his Catalina Island marionette show three years earlier, had left puppetry to become a cameraman for Disney's *Snow White and the Seven Dwarfs*. When Walt Disney heard that Jones was a puppeteer, he put him to work building models of the animator's designs for *Pinocchio*. Jones built the first Pinocchio marionette around 1938.

Bob contacted Jones, and was invited to see what was happening at the studio. Jones explained that he was part of a special unit that was exploring the use of puppets for upcoming features. A few years later, Bob found himself working as an advisor to Walt Disney for puppetry projects.

Bob saw Disney again in 1940 at *Dumbo*, another Disney puppet production by Wayne Barlow for J.W. Robinson's. Bob had helped Barlow build the puppets, and was also working as a performer. For each production of *Snow White* and *Dumbo*, the puppeteers had filmed a special prologue to the show to introduce the puppets. At a special preview, Bob sat next to Disney and his brother, Roy. During the prologue, Walt turned to his brother and said, "When did our studio film that?" Roy replied, "We didn't." Bob quickly explained how he and the others had filmed the fade-outs by turning the lights away from the camera, and other simple effects. "We gotta remember to do that," Walt said to Roy. "We could save the studio a lot of money!" He was impressed with Bob's talents and determination.

In 1952, design work began for the Disneyland theme park, with construction starting in 1954. The park officially opened in 1955. Because of Bob's expertise in window display, Walt Disney asked him to make product sales exhibits for Disneyland's store windows.

Bob's letters reached Walt Disney at his studio on Hyperion Avenue. Opposite: Bob Bromley's scrapbook of his Snow White puppet show from the late 1930s. The show was originally presented at Robinson's, and Disney provided the soundtrack.

PRODUCTION BY WAYNE BARLOW AND MYSELF, SKETCHES AND SOUND TRACK FURNISHED BY DISNEY.

INTRODUCTION WAS FILMED, IN COLOR AND BLENDED INTO OPENING SCENE.

REVOLVING STAGE IN THEATRE BUILT FOR US BY ROBINSONS DEPT. STORE.

Working alongside Morton Haack, Bob helped design quite a few set pieces for early displays in the park. One of his proudest achievements was a set of cut-out jesters he made to hold items for sale. These jesters debuted in the windows of the Fantasy of Disneyland shop in Fantasyland. The wooden harlequins held anything from necklaces and clothing, to their speciality: marionettes for sale. These same jesters now proudly welcome visitors to the new Bob Baker Marionette Theater in Highland Park.

Walt Disney realized the value of puppets, having already seen the popularity of Mickey Mouse increase due to the Hestwood Marionettes, not to mention Barlow's well-attended Disney shows. It's no wonder that some of Bob's early commercial puppets also found homes in Disneyland shop windows. Disney even considered having a marionette theater on Disneyland grounds. "One day," Bob recalled, "Walt called me into a room that had quite a movie set, complete with palm trees and castles. [Walt said,] 'It's going to be Disneyland. Why don't you put a puppet theater in there?'"

However, to perform at Disneyland, Bob would have had to become a corporate sponsor at the park, which he could not afford at that time. That didn't keep him from making numerous contributions to the look of Disneyland. As an advisor for special projects, when *Babes in Toyland* debuted in 1961, Bob helped design the Toyland Village exhibit in the park, as well as costumes and floats used for that year's park-wide parade, "Fantasy on Parade."

Bob Mills's Disneyland puppet shows featuring peppermint guitarists and candy skaters, soon to become beloved on Bob Baker's stage. Opposite: Characters from the *101 Dalmatians* displays from the Disneyland windows. The sets were built by Disney artists, with figures and props built by Bob Baker Studio. 1972.

Although Bob did not open a puppet theater at Disneyland, his good friend Bob Mills did. When the Fantasy of Disneyland store became the Tinker Bell Toy Shoppe in 1957, the company that ran the Main Street Emporium managed them both. They thought a marionette attraction in the Fantasyland Theater would be great alongside the new store. The Emporium had deeper pockets than Bob did, and was therefore able to finance another attraction within the park; they just had to hire the puppeteer. Walt Disney had seen Mills perform at Children's Fairyland in Oakland, and he offered him the job. It's quite a coincidence that Bob was also a mentor to a young Mills.

Disney finally had a puppet show at Disneyland for five years, until Mills moved on to become a film makeup technician, and the theater space was converted to merchandise display space. Mills sold all of his puppets that had been made for the Disneyland show to the Bob Baker Marionette Theater in 1962, and to this day they still perform for cheering youngsters. The famous trio of Bob Baker Birthday Dogs are Mills's creations, as well as many of the puppets in *Nutcracker* and other fantasy numbers.

Since opening day, the decorative and often-animated windows of the Main Street Emporium have been a popular attraction at Disneyland. Sometimes they feature a new product, and other times they are themed to feature films and their popular characters. Before Walt Disney passed away in 1966, he proposed that every seven or so years, his animated films should be re-released in movie theaters. (He did not, however, want them made available for public sale. That changed years later, under new leadership.) In 1969, *Peter Pan* was re-released for the third time, and Disneyland wanted to celebrate it in a special way. Remembering Bob's work, and his excellent window dressings, the Walt Disney Company asked him to build animated puppets for the Main Street Emporium. Each window was designed by the Disney crew, and Bob supplied the mechanical puppet characters.

To make the figures lighter and easier to move with motors, Baker built the puppets out of foam and lightweight plastic; very little wood was used. The heads were produced using an expensive process of vacuum-forming a plastic-like foam. Once they had hardened, they were sanded and hand-painted. The bodies and hands were sculpted out of foam under the direction of Bob Baker artist King Hall. The Disney company supplied animator's drawings and model sheets that were used to create the Disney look. Once the figures were finished, they were installed in the windows, where the sets had already been constructed by Disney carpenters and artists.

The *Peter Pan* attraction was a huge success and set the standard for the next five years of Disneyland windows that Bob produced. When viewed in succession, the windows presented key moments from the film. Once the displays were done with, they were stored for future use. Because the mechanical figures were made of fragile foam, they had a limited shelf life. Bob once said that Michael Jackson purchased the largest of these window displays, where the miniature Darling children flew and circled over the streets of London and Neverland. He preserved it and had it installed at his Neverland Ranch.

Other animated windows followed in successive years: *Sleeping Beauty* in 1970, and both *The Aristocats* and *Bedknobs and Broomsticks* in 1971. Bob created his final set of windows, featuring *101 Dalmatians*, in 1972. For the Dalmatian dogs, the Bob Baker artists had to draw each individual spot on the figures with a black marking pen after the puppets had been flocked. Disney World so admired the windows in California that they asked Bob to recreate them at their location in Florida. In 1973, Bob installed new windows for *Sleeping Beauty* at Disney World, and a new *Bedknobs and Broomsticks* series in 1974. Visiting

Opposite: Nearly exact recreations of iconic scenes from *101 Dalmations* were recreated in Bob's window displays. Scale drawings were made for each of these figures, which still reside in the Bob Baker archives at the theater. Above: Flora, Fauna, and Merryweather (the Three Good Fairies from *Sleeping Beauty*) and the Queen (left) are housed in the Bob Baker workshop before heading over to Disneyland.

Disney World years later, Bob was asked by a director to come and see the most beautiful things ever produced for the theme park. Bob was surprised and touched to see that his puppets for *Sleeping Beauty* were still in use.

As a tribute to Bob for his work at Disneyland, in 1983 the Disney Imagineers included some of his commercial puppets in the New Fantasyland and the Pinocchio's Daring Journey ride. Eagle-eyed fans can find his Dutch Boy and Girl, Ballerina, and Coco the Clown hanging in the rafters of the final scene in Geppetto's workshop, before exiting the attraction.

But Disneyland wasn't done with Bob's puppet-making skills. In early 1984, he was asked to create a special Pinocchio marionette that would be sold at the Disneyana store in honor of the *Pinocchio* theater re-release. The Bob Baker artists produced 2,500 collectible Pinocchio puppets, hand-carved out of wood with loving care. This was the beginning of the Disneyana Gallery's Disney Marionette Collection Limited Editions. From 1982 to 1989, Bob produced classic Disney marionettes that sold in Disney art galleries, Disneyana, and the Disney Store. Between 1992 and 1993, he also produced other Disney marionettes that could only be purchased directly through the Disneyana store catalogue.

Bob was careful to comply with Walt's exacting standards, to ensure that his marionettes would join the ranks of the fine craftsmanship of Walt Disney-licensed products. Each piece of Bob's puppets began with an examination of Disney artist renderings and model sheets. Next, mechanical drawings detected where strings should be placed, and where movement would make sense for the

Puppets from the Disney classic characters collection. The marionettes were in production from 1982 to 1989. Opposite, far right: Pluto, Donald, Horace, and Clarabelle are reproductions of Hestwood Marionettes.

puppet. Each moving part was finely sculpted: hands, feet, heads, bodies, and so forth. The sculpted parts were then cast, with molds created for reproducing the many pieces. . These pieces were refined and studied for authenticity, durability, and perfection. The final process included detailed painting, replica costuming, and stringing. All marionettes came with a certificate of authenticity and a card featuring marionette design concept sketches. "Made especially for The Disney Company by the Bob Baker Marionettes," read a numbered metal plaque on the control.

In total, the Bob Baker Marionette Theater created thirty-seven collectible marionettes for the park, including characters from the early Disney cartoons like Mickey, Minnie, Pluto, Donald, Clarabelle Cow, Horace Horsecollar, Bucky and June Bug, and favorites from *Snow White*, *Pinocchio*, *Sleeping Beauty*, and *The Nightmare Before Christmas*.

When Disney decided to release *Pinocchio* on VHS, Bob was asked to make 200 life-sized, fifty-four-inch marionettes for a special promotion across America. The first 200 video stores that sold the most Disney videos would each receive one of the giant Pinocchio marionettes. These puppets are rare, and often fetch thousands of dollars when sold at auction today. Bob also made life-sized marionettes of "Mickey at 60," as well as Sorcerer Mickey from *Fantasia*, for private sales.

Other puppets were created that were never released to Disney fans. A Big Bad Wolf was considered too scary for youngsters, and a "flip puppet" of the Evil Queen and Witch from *Snow White* was abandoned. This marionette was manipulated by pulling one of two control bars, which would flip the puppet over and change her from the Queen to the Witch and back again. Bob also wanted to release Peter Pan, Captain Hook, and Tinker Bell in the *Peter Pan* series, and Cruella de Vil from *101 Dalmatians*. Only Tinker Bell and Hook ever made it to a final prototype stage, but they were never produced for sale.

In 1998, Bob once again began building smaller versions of his Disney marionettes for the Walt Disney Gallery. Each character had an edition of 1,000 to 1,500 pieces. These smaller ten-inch puppets, which were more affordable since they cost under $100, were sold through the

Disney Store catalogue. Included in this set of puppets was a collection of five Mickey Mouses celebrating "70 Happy Years!," as well as three Minnies, several Donalds, a Pluto, and a Goofy. All of the elegantly designed figures featured rubber-tube arms and legs, and beautifully sewn costumes. The new Disney puppets were easily identifiable by the marionette stands that came with each one, and included a brass nameplate prominently displaying the character's name and the fact that they were a Bob Baker Marionette.

In 2007, Bob was asked to produce an authentic replica of the original Pinocchio marionette made by Bob Jones, which the *Pinocchio* animators had used to study movement. Throughout the process of animation design, the final animated puppet had undergone a few subtle changes from the first maquette marionette. After filming was completed, the sculpted model of the marionette's head was presented to Bob, whose work Walt Disney so deeply admired. In 2003, Jones's original marionette was discovered hidden away in a cabinet that was filled with Disney paraphernalia, which had been blocked by telephone equipment and wires. Working in conjunction with the Walt Disney Showcase Collection and Mr. Replicas (a company widely known for producing high-quality reproductions of famous movie and cult-classic memorabilia), the workshop set about building 1,940 limited-edition marionettes to honor the film's original 1940 release date. This newest version of Disney's puppet is very similar to the first one made by Bob for the Disneyana Galleries in 1984. The major differences were the casting and new paint job of the

A multitude of Disney characters could often be seen hanging in the theater's workshop. Characters from *The Nightmare Before Christmas* (top) were the last edition produced in this collectible series. Opposite: Bob Baker with his commemorative fifty-four-inch Pinocchio, and Yellow Cat on his lap.

older puppet head, longer wooden joint pins protruding from the arms and legs, and a marionette stand for display. This newer version was sold by many outlets, and was therefore more readily available to the general public.

In addition to *Bedknobs and Broomsticks* and *Escape to Witch Mountain*, Bob Baker Marionettes worked on many other projects for the Disney corporation. For Disney Video, Bob designed a casket that resembled the Queen's in *Snow White*, to hold and display Disney VHS tapes. In 1983, Bob and company helped animate and build smaller versions of Figment the Dragon, the mascot of the Imagination! pavilion at Epcot Center, that were filmed for use with the Journey Into Your Imagination ride. And when Splash Mountain opened at Disneyland in 1989, Bob and his artists made a life-size Brer Rabbit puppet that acted as emcee for the opening of the attraction. The Bob Baker Marionette Theater has also filmed and produced many segments for *The Wonderful World of Disney* television series.

Bob continued to work as an advisor for Disney films, and was known as *the* person to call whenever park puppet figures were needed for display or private sale. As part of Bob's legacy, his artistry is held in high esteem by Disney animators and Imagineers. The theater continues to have a close and celebrated relationship with Disney.

Bob Baker fabricated a Figment puppet that was featured prominently in the final video scenes of the 1983 Epcot ride "Journey into Imagination." According to Tony Baxter, the former senior vice president of creative development at Walt Disney Imagineering, Figment was "originally slated for... animation. The studio was overworked and funds were getting tight. It was decided to try puppets." Animatronics from the ride are pictured in Polaroid photos.

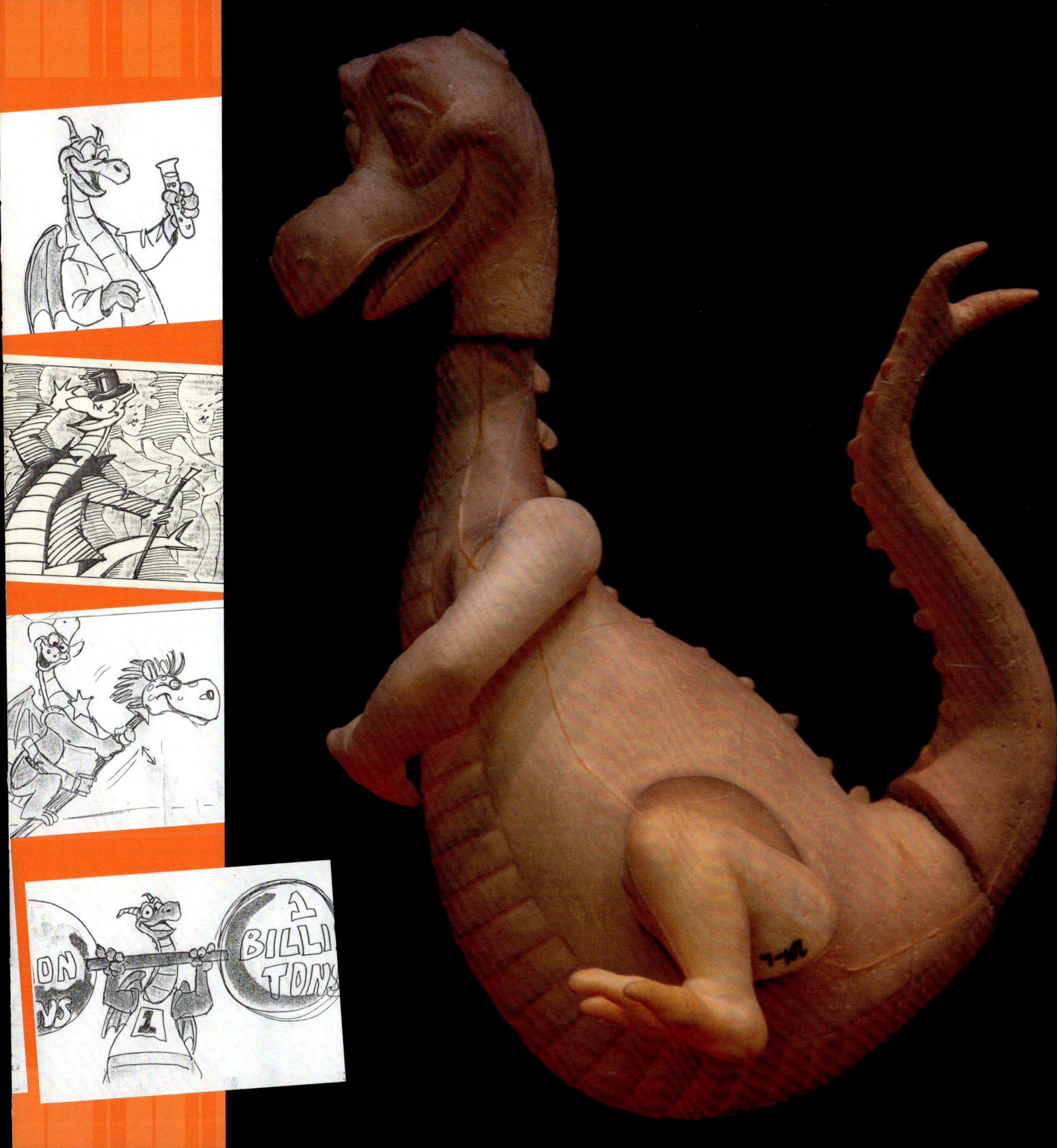
1
BILLI
TONS

In L.A. to Stay

The 1980s and 1990s were challenging years for the Bob Baker Marionette Theater. The times were changing, technology was changing, and tightened school budgets no longer supported as many children's activities, or what some considered "frivolous" field trips. Foot traffic never improved; the surrounding neighborhood saw a fair amount of crime, which did not help draw young families, tourists, and tour companies into the theater's parking lot.

But for the people who lived in the community, there was something magical about having the Bob Baker Marionette Theater in their neighborhood. The whole building was an enchanted white canvas, with glittery sparkles added to its paint. Graffiti and broken windows may have scarred the buildings surrounding the theater, but no one painted or abused Bob's fairytale structure. The community took extra special pride in this place. Bob cared about the community, too; he would hire from the neighborhood first, and he never turned away children who couldn't afford the price of a ticket. Generations of kids grew up with Bob's puppets, and when they were teens, many joined the theater as technical help, puppet builders, or even puppeteers. When they moved on, their own children became a part of Bob's company. Bob treated everyone as an equal. He received hundreds of awards from social organizations in recognition of his work with children and families, as well as his efforts to employ theater workers from his local community. Bob worked magic not only in the theater, but also in the hearts of the people that surrounded him.

Even though Bob had community accolades and support, his financial troubles accrued. After fifty-one years as a professional puppeteer—twenty-five of those running the

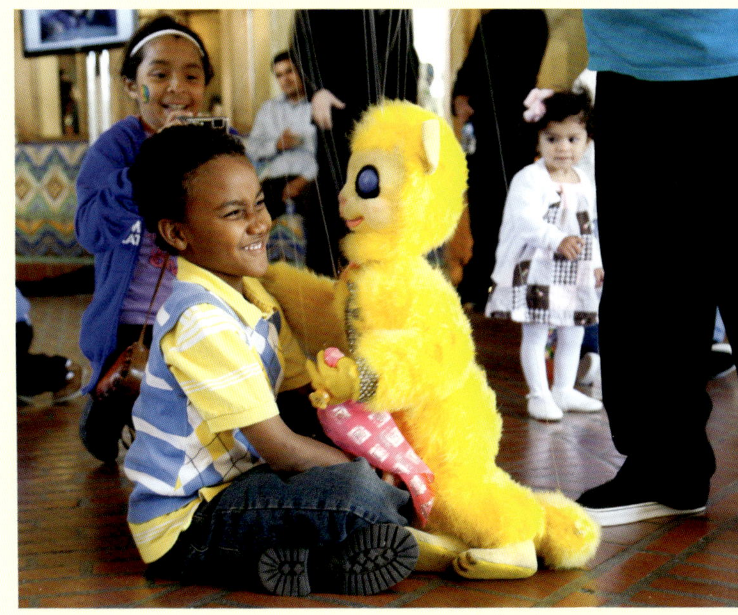

Opposite: Marionettes from Bob's original *Circus!* production continue to delight and enchant audiences nearly half a century after its original presentation. Above: Yellow Cat greets a child.

marionette theater—Bob began thinking about retirement or that he might pursue other endeavors. His partner, Alton, was thinking the same thing. Bob was sixty-four at the time, and Alton was seventy-six. The theater had accumulated massive debt over the decades, and the partners had mortgaged their personal real estate and the theater property many times to make ends meet.

Then, as if in a fairytale, Don Battjes, a fellow puppeteer and a director of corporate real estate and facility management, offered to buy the Bob Baker Marionette Theater to ensure that Bob's legacy would continue. Battjes had admired Bob's work since he had met him and Alton at a puppeteer's convention as a teen. Battjes had taken up puppetry as a childhood hobby, which led to him study theater design, fine arts, and architecture at Hope College in Michigan and L'Ecole d'Architecture in Fontainebleau, France. After graduation, he was hooked. He returned to Michigan and launched the Donald Battjes Puppets with his wife, Anne. Eight successful years later, he settled in California in the 1970s and rekindled his friendship with Bob and Alton. Battjes had also been an executive for Crocker Bank, 20th Century Fox, and MDP, Ltd., a subsidiary of Hughes Aircraft. But the marionette theater combined a lot of his interests—business, musical theater, stage production, and set design.

Trusting that Battjes would carry on their legacy, in 1988 Bob and Alton sold the theater to Battjes and his partner, Doug Young, who formed a new company called Bob Baker Puppets, Inc. Battjes and

Don Battjes (top) is responsible for much of the interior of the refurbished Bob Baker Marionette Theater (opposite), including designated red carpet seating space and painted curtain walls. Left: While Don renovated the theater, Bob continued to perform on the road with Tom Ray.

ON THE AIR

Spotlight on Talent

Ursula Heinle

Born and raised in Germany during World War II, Ursula Heinle emigrated to America and became a fashion model. She later worked as a dressmaker for the designer James Galanos, and became known for her intricate handiwork and attention to detail. She made dresses for the Hollywood elite, including Nancy Reagan's gown at Ronald Reagan's presidential inaugural ball. Her first job for Bob was creating the elaborate tuxedo adorning the Disney "Mickey at 60" collectible. For thirty years, she fashioned the marionette costumes for the theater as well as for the Disney Collectible Marionettes. In particular, her work can still be seen on the marionette clowns in the opening sequence for *Nutcracker*.

Young now found themselves at the helm of the Bob Baker Marionette Theater and studio, with a company of more than twenty craftspeople and a collection of 2,000 characters on strings.

After they sold the theater, Bob and Alton decided to take a much-needed vacation to Europe. The two had complete confidence in the abilities of Battjes and Young. When Bob returned from Europe, he and his roadshow partner, Tom Ray, still performed marionette shows at fairs and clubs for the theater. Battjes hoped to maintain the quality and charm of the theater and its productions, but wanted to bring it into "the next generation." By the 1980s, the musical numbers, which came from the 1950s and 1960s, were becoming dated. The lighting and sound needed improvement, and the interior space required new paint and carpeting. The theater's accounting was still done by hand, without the use of a computer. Battjes invested thousands in an effort to reduce the accumulated debt of the business. He never had any plans to expand to a larger theater space, just to improve the one that existed.

And so, the innovations began in earnest. One of Battjes's first decisions was to hire a business manager to set up a new system of accounting. Cash flow was leaking, and the business needed to build better relationships with vendors and establish a more efficient box office system. The workshop, the scenery, puppet storage, and the crew of puppet artists—were all removed from the former theater and re-established at a new facility in Highland Park.

John Leland was tasked with designing a new party room where the old workshop used to be, as well as providing a new look for the theater's interior. The walls were painted to look like curtains, and a new carpet was installed, along with risers for chairs on all sides. As Leland worked on creating the iconic look of the Bob Baker Marionette Theater, Battjes began designing new programs, scripts, and musical scores that would blend the talents of a new group of young theatrical interns with the nostalgia of older puppeteers—a combination that would appeal to a broader audience. Trying to disprove the old adage that "puppetry is just for kids," Battjes branded all of his promotions with the banner headline "Entertainment for All Ages!"

Battjes also quickly realized that the twenty-six-inch Disney marionettes currently being sold by the theater were too expensive, with a price tag of $400 to $600 per puppet. A smaller, more affordable product was needed. Ursula Heinle developed a new ten-inch design that was smaller and more affordable, with only seven strings. Instead of wood-machined arms and legs (unless they were absolutely needed), Battjes developed puppets that used rubber tube animation, much like the old cartoon characters looked like in the 1920s and 1930s. The new marionettes could be made simpler, faster, and at a lower cost, allowing more parents to buy them for their children. With the design of the smaller puppets, Battjes signed new manufacturing contracts with Disney and Warner Bros., who carried them in their respective company stores. He eventually moved all of his manufacturing to South China, where he fashioned a European Collection of small marionettes for sale. These became known as Parade Street Marionettes, exclusively distributed by the Toy Corporation of America.

During this time, Bob's name and presence at the theater were very important. Battjes had purchased all of the theater's physical assets, which included the puppets, the building, the land, and the intellectual properties, which included the Bob Baker name. Battjes had no wish to start over as a new company. Change is always difficult, and a lot of the nuances were hard for Bob and his former staff to swallow. Battjes's new production staff wanted the freedom to create, while remaining respectful of the

One of Don Battjes biggest changes was designing the party room and workshop. Pictured here is the party room as it looked until the theater's last performance in 2018.

THE
BOB BAKER
MARIONETTE
THEATER

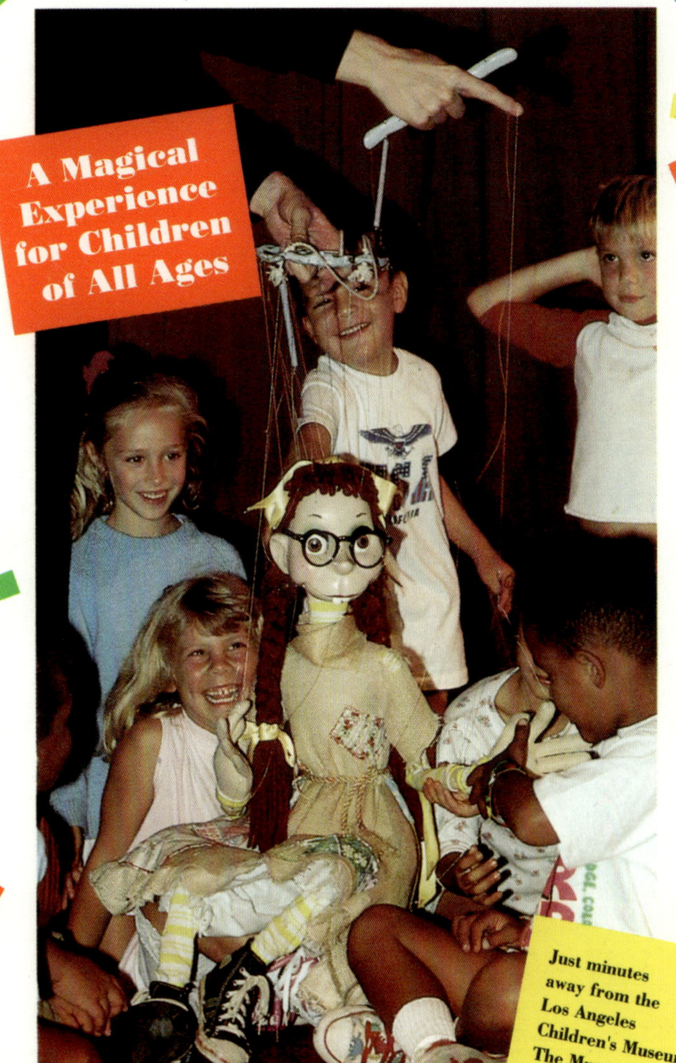

Just minutes away from the Los Angeles Children's Museum, The Museum of Contemporary Art, Olvera Street, Chinatown, Dodger Stadium and Lawry's California Center, the Theater can be the highlight of a fun-filled day in downtown Los Angeles.

Spend a wonderful afternoon in a fantasy world filled with ice-skating polar bears, musical chimney sweeps, sugar plum fairies, surfboarding clowns...you never know what you'll encounter at Southern California's most unique entertainment experience: The Bob Baker Marionette Theater.

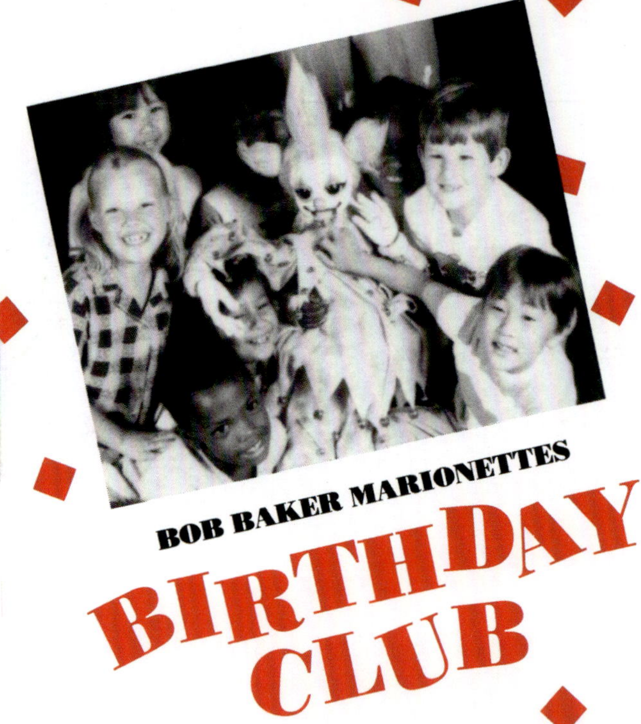

existing culture at Bob's theater. Opinions about Battjes varied widely; the stories portrayed him as either a devil or an angel, and, depending on the viewpoint, he was either vilified or glorified.

Young and Battjes determined that, rather than doing two productions a year, the business should try for four. In addition to reviving old favorites, Battjes and his artists created three new "Don Battjes Entertainments." The first was a newer production of *The Nutcracker* that was based on the show Battjes had created when he began his puppetry career. The next year, the theater produced an elaborate *Snow Queen*, and ended the following year with a complex adventure called *Song of Scheherazade*.

Although the new shows were ambitious and intriguing, the general public missed the old Bob Baker magic. They loved the changes made to the theater and party room, but were more critical of Battjes's new productions. The only positive note in one reviewer's comments focused on Bob's trademark stylings: "The element that has always worked for the company still exists: a colorful, comic variety of quirky puppets on parade that perch on delighted young audience members' knees, kiss a cheek, or pirouette tantalizingly near."

After three years, Battjes and Young threw in the towel, citing the theater's poor marginal profitability. They asked Bob and Alton if they wanted to buy back the theater and business. During their time away from the theater, Bob and Alton had realized that the marionettes were their passion and legacy, and they had regretted handing them off to anyone else. Afraid that the theater would close forever, Bob and Alton agreed to buy back the properties by July 1991.

Although Bob and Alton were exceptional artists and designers of their craft, truth be told, they often found themselves struggling with business decisions. The theater would always need an infusion of cash, a good business manager, and a way to somehow cap extravagant spending. That is one reason why Battjes was convinced the theater would always struggle financially.

When Bob returned to stewardship of the theater, he focused on the importance of protecting his legacy. Feeling his age and the recent loss of the business, he wanted to ensure that the Bob Baker Marionettes would continue to entertain future generations. He came up with many new ideas, including designing new collectible marionettes and creating a school for puppetry and dramatic arts in conjunction with the theater.

Bob was back in charge of the theater just in time for the Christmas season, his favorite time of the year. Over the decades, the holiday show at the Bob Baker Marionette Theater had always been a highlight. The audience came expecting the dazzling holiday spectacle of Santa's workshop or dancing reindeer, along with the ever-pleasing additions of Chanukah acts. Bob often included elaborate city scenes in the productions, with puppets ice skating to music supplied by a Dickensian band of marionette musicians and carolers. Holiday productions included *Holiday Hoop de Dooh*, *'Tis the Season*, *Holiday Fiesta*, *A Surprise Package*, and *The Holiday Adventures of Hansel and Gretel*. Watching a Bob Baker Christmas show is like witnessing, as a child, the holiday windows of department stores coming alive, holding the audience spellbound with their movement. Bob just loved Christmas. Today, more than ever, the Christmas season is very important to the Bob Baker Marionette Theater. The theater's yuletide show, as well as its many

Opposite: Birthday parties at the theater were a consistent hallmark throughout the years, with giant lollipops, gold crowns, and puppet gifts for the guest of honor. Above: The 1980s saw a dramatic increase in the size of marionettes—Mr. and Mrs. Claus are some of the heaviest puppets, at approximately twenty pounds each.

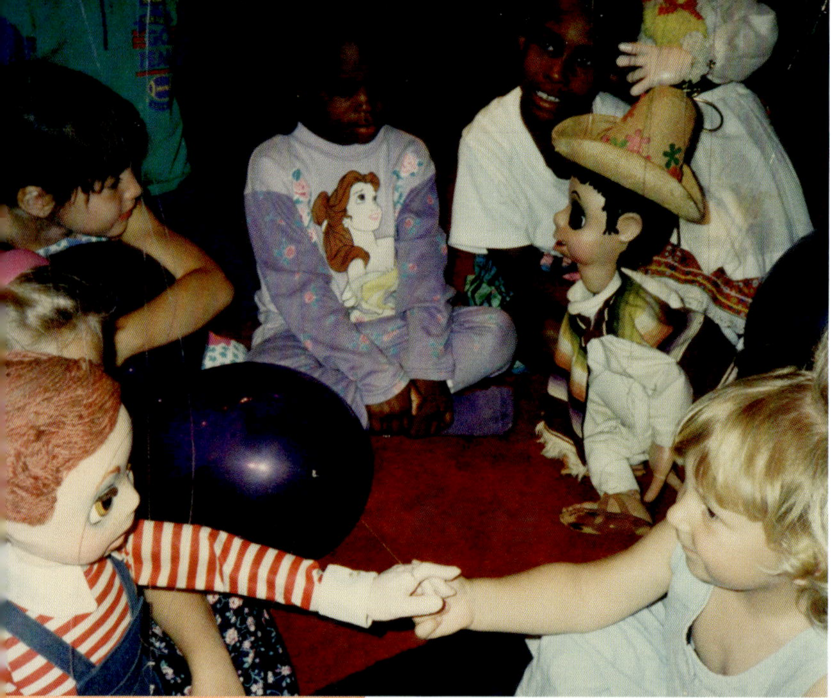

holiday puppet showings at parties, festivals, and schools, provides a significant annual revenue boost.

For the holiday show in his first year back at the theater, Bob decided to revisit his *Nutcracker* production and completely revamp his earlier ideas. Whereas his first *Nutcracker* tale had been performed mainly with hand-and-rod puppets, Bob decided now was the time for a marionette version of the tale. Set designer John Leland, costumer Ursula Heinle, and a new apprentice named Matt Scott began visualizing the tale in a modern way, using updated scenic effects, magical musical interludes, and unusual styles of puppetry to portray the dreamlike settings. "We built this business on quality, and we'll try to put the quality back in!" Alton declared.

The new *Nutcracker* proved to be very popular, and became a signature show for the Bob Baker Marionette Theater. But before the season was over, the reality of the following year and its expenses began knocking on the door. Alton quickly closed down the Highland Park workshop and brought everything back to the original theater location, taking inventory to ensure that everything was accounted for. He just hoped that quality did not come with too high a price tag. Alas, Alton soon found out that the theater was in need of a quick cash influx of $25,000, due to unpaid insurance premiums and other bills. The recession of the early 1990s had made freelance puppet jobs harder to book, creating a perfect storm.

The Bob Baker Marionettes turned to the community for help. While Bob was creating the new *Nutcracker* production, Alton worked to cover salaries

As time marched forward, the theater played host to multiple generations of Angelenos—the children of the children who attended the original performances in the 1960s. Opposite: Don Battjes made significant changes to the exterior of the theater as well, including this yellow brick road.

BOB BAKER
MARIONETTE
THEATER
NOW PLAYING
A SPECIAL
SHOW!

and expenses. Newspaper and magazine articles detailed the theater's need to fundraise in order to stay open. Community organizations and individuals in Los Angeles banded together to cover the bills—the first of many times such support would be needed.

Bob believed that the best way to secure financial independence for the theater was to dramatically expand its reach. He envisioned an organization called the Academy of Puppetry and Allied Arts, which would house a puppetry school, workshops, and even a restaurant. Bob and Alton hoped to raise funds to purchase and refurbish the rundown buildings near the theater. He hoped the new school and related construction would create jobs and new business in the community. Bob said, "It's a theatrical project, yes, but we'd teach puppetry along with all of the other things. There would be art classes. There would be drama classes. Acting classes, body movement classes—learning how to move your body as a dancer. That's what I want to teach here. It's a dream. It's a dream that hasn't become a nightmare, but it's a dream. You have to have an idea, then you've got to picture it . . . whether it will be, or not, is how strong I get other people to picture it, too."

At the time, though, Bob found himself with a unique situation. Most of his previous puppet builders and professional puppeteers had either moved on or passed away. In earlier days, he had always filled these positions with qualified, trained individuals. Unfortunately, at this time, Bob didn't have the money to pay experienced artists. But he soon saw a shift in his work force that was going to create the foundation for the next generation of staff. Bob had always hired from the community, and looked for people who had grown up with and loved the puppets. The jobs they filled were "maintenance"—running the lights and spotlight, and creating that special feeling after a performance when the hosts served refreshments and ice cream to the theater visitors.

But then a "flip" began to occur. As Bob was distracted by financial troubles, the maintenance staff started helping in the workshop, stringing and repairing puppets, creating costumes, even making new marionettes. The existing puppeteers began to take on teens from the community as apprentices. The new staff started to energize the theater with new ideas and possibilities.

Above: Alton, Tina Gainsboro, and Bob celebrate their return to the theater circa 1992. Opposite: The backstage bays of the theater house an elaborate lighting system of coffee-can lights and theater effects that represent decades of stagecraft technology. Puppeteers often run lights and drops in addition to puppets, running backstage to make adjustments or turn on a blacklight before grabbing a puppet to perform.

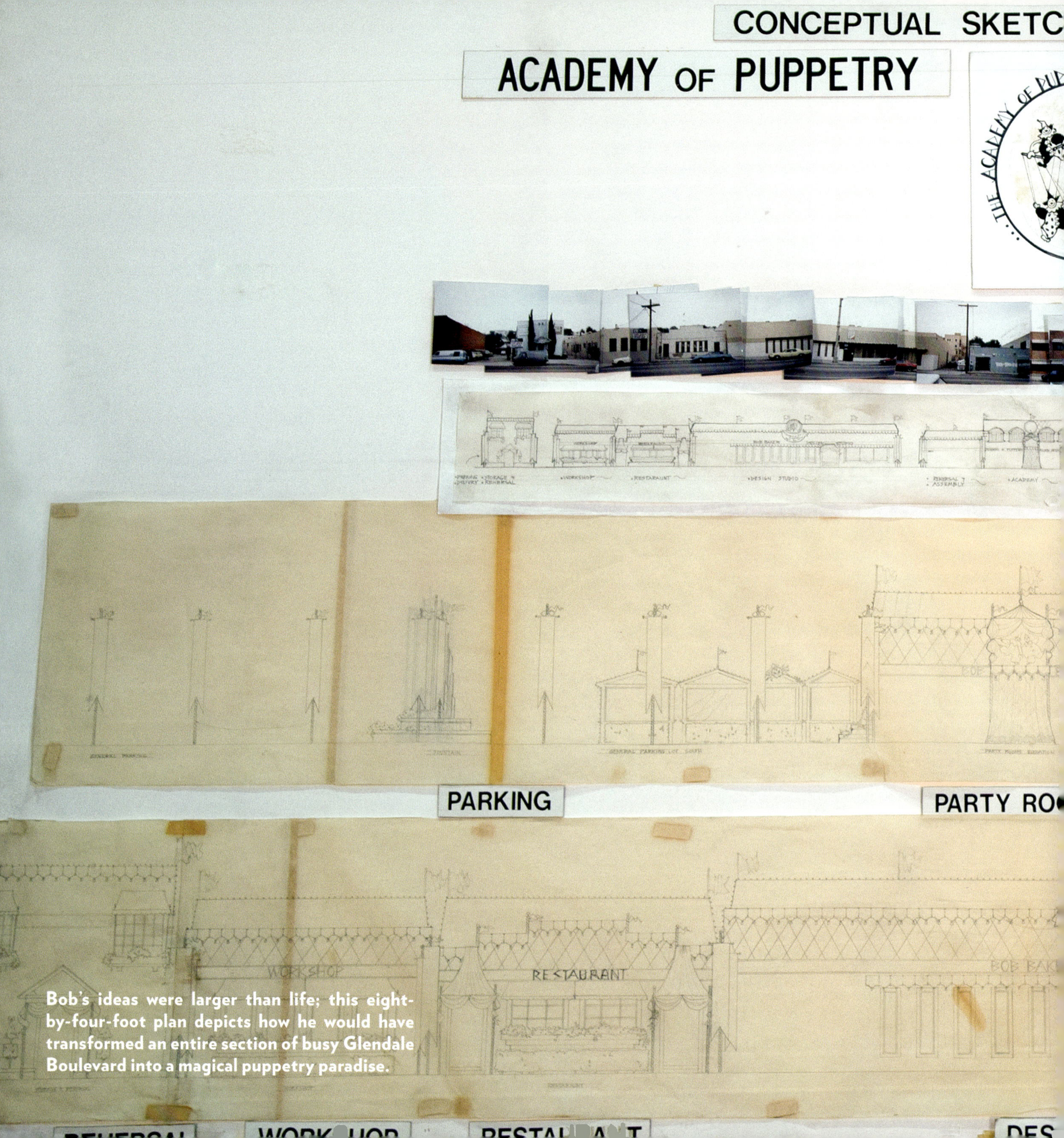

Bob's ideas were larger than life; this eight-by-four-foot plan depicts how he would have transformed an entire section of busy Glendale Boulevard into a magical puppetry paradise.

FOR THE PROPOSED
AND ALLIED ARTS
A NON PROFIT CORPORATION
MARIONETTE
THEATER
THEATER
OFFICES
PARKING

Bob once said, "I think my ideas are kind of big. And my pocketbook is small." The theater was always looking for new opportunities to increase revenue. Bob was never happy with Battjes's changes to the workshop, party room, and theater space. But he did, begrudgingly, come to love Battjes's small commercial marionettes. Bob hoped that manufacturing and selling the commercial marionettes would help make up the lost revenue from smaller audiences. He decided to create a larger store display, where patrons could buy Bob Baker Marionette products after the show as they enjoyed ice cream and coffee.

As time wore on, Bob's fantasy-like theater on 1345 West 1st Street stayed true to the type of entertainment families expected from the Bob Baker Marionette Theater. And even though it continued to deliver on quality and fun, audiences were still not arriving in the large numbers needed to keep that quality assured.

The theater suffered a loss on October 9, 2001, when Alton Wood, Bob's longtime partner and sage, passed away. At the time of Alton's death, the duo had just celebrated fifty-two years of making children's dreams come true. Alton had handled the business side of things so Bob could deal directly with the artistic side. Now, Bob found himself juggling both paints and paychecks.

For most of the theater's history, Bob had been firmly and definitely in charge of all aspects of the theater. But after Alton passed, and as Bob grew older, he could no longer manage every aspect of a busy theater on his own. Whether he wanted to or not, he needed to allow other people to take some control. Bob's time was spread thin, and support was needed. Fortunately, at this time, the theater was finding itself at the center of renewed attention from the community; the internet had helped a new generation of fans discover this hidden gem. With increased attendance at the shows, a younger public began to learn about this classic form of entertainment. Returning to the theater they had once attended as children, the nostalgic audience experienced the same joy they had felt many years before, and were eager to preserve it for the next generation. They saw how much help was needed and, for the first time in the theater's history, volunteers were able to jump in and offer their assistance.

In 2007, a new staff member, Alex Evans arrived at the theater. He had found Bob through a Google search for "Los Angeles puppetry," and quickly fell in love with every aspect of the theater. Evans began by helping Bob in the library, digitizing the music and moving the theater into a technological era. He started training to become a puppeteer and was one of the last to train directly under Bob. He took on increasing responsibility for running and developing the theater.

Despite its new popularity, the business was still struggling to get out of the enormous debt that had accrued. There was now serious talk about the theater actually closing. In an effort to protect the theater from closure and secure its future in the community as a historic landmark, the Los Angeles Conservancy's Historic Theatre Committee nominated it and worked tirelessly to secure its designation as a Historic-Cultural Monument. Members of the Los Angeles Puppetry Guild marched on the chambers of Los Angeles City Hall with their puppets dancing and prancing around the council members, hoping to have the Bob Baker Marionette Theater declared a Los Angeles monument. Bob's Coco the Clown was even seen in the crowd. In recognition of its association with pioneering puppeteer Bob Baker, and its significant role in the development of the art of puppetry, the theater building was designated as Historic-Cultural Monument #958 on June 3, 2009, by the Los Angeles City Council. The final vote count? Unanimous, 14–0.

Despite this honor, the theater's financial trouble began to take its toll. Bob had mortgaged his house to raise funds for the theater, and by this time, the bank was threatening to evict him from his home and force a sale of the theater building. In a drastic effort to increase revenue, Bob agreed to sell at auction a majority of the film and television puppets stored in the theater's archives, including original puppets, design renderings, and prototypes that were normally only brought out for museum displays. On December 1, 2011, Julien's Auctions organized the sale of marionettes and puppets that had appeared in *G.I. Blues*, *Wild, Wild West*, *Close Encounters of the Third Kind*, *A Star Is Born*, and many other classic film and television puppet performances. The marionettes found new homes in the personal and public collections of numerous movie fans. But the emotional loss of the puppets far outweighed the small financial gain of their sale; the funds generated by the auction barely offset Bob's debt, and couldn't compare to the pricelessness of

Opposite: Puppetry Guild members pose in front of Los Angeles City Hall after the theater is approved for Historic-Cultural Monument consideration in 2009. Above: Alex Evans shows off his Wiz Clown tattoo.

the puppets. After this experience, Bob and the theater's remaining staff swore to never sell its assets again.

In mid-June of 2013, the bills finally came due. In order to avoid foreclosure, Bob realized it was time to sell the theater building and surrounding land. His health was slowly declining, and he and his partner, Richard Shuler, decided this was the only thing to do. "For sale" signs were placed around the property, but they mysteriously kept disappearing. This business was the heart of the community, and had changed the lives of so many of its residents; no one wanted the dream to fade.

After unsuccessfully pursuing many buyers who might keep the theater on as a tenant, on September 9, 2013, the building was bought by real estate developer Eli Elimelech for $1.3 million. On the property, Elimelech planned to build "Beverly Terrace," a seven-story, 102-unit apartment building. Initial plans for the construction included bulldozing the theater's office, kitchen, storage area, and workshop. However, Elimelech planned to keep the large performance space intact and allow the theater to continue operating on the property until construction began—the only offer Bob had received that would allow the shows to continue, even if temporarily.

Despite these challenges, Bob remained hopeful. "It's nothing to be depressed about if you look at it in one way," he said at the time. "Whatever is going to be good will be good, and can be better than what it is. I'll tell you, we've done a lot of nice things. We've entertained a lot of children. We've made a lot of children happy. I've entertained elderly people and made it a very happy moment in their lives. So, if nothing else, we've done that. We haven't made a lot of money—although, what's a lot of money? If you don't use it right, you might as well not bother. Somebody, somewhere along the line, is going to help us. I may not be alive to see it, but it's going to come. It's going to happen!"

Bob Baker passed away of natural causes on November 28, 2014, at the age of ninety. Surrounded by his friends and family, he kept his dream of a better tomorrow alive through his words and actions. "So it's the end of an era," he reflected. "It's gone . . . it's changed. I'm hoping that everyone will be able to carry on. Make something of it. It's yours now. Bless you all! Bye-bye."

And the show did go on—the very next day. The staff that was left at the Bob Baker Marionette Theater decided to make sure there would always be a show. Some said the lights flickered strangely, but the puppeteers refused to dim them or let the spots lose their brightness. Bob's life was a celebration, and all of those whom he had believed in and given purpose to, from the craftsmen to the puppeteers, joined together to help keep the marionettes moving.

Above: The Black Cat and the Money Cats perform at the theater. Opposite: After he passed, Bob was remembered in publications and tributes across Los Angeles—from the *Los Angeles Times* to *Variety* to the thousands of messages from individuals impacted by his puppets, theater, and performances over the years.

A last hurrah before the theater's big move brought together Bob Baker staff, friends, puppeteers, and supporters.

BAKER MARIONETTE THEATER
NOW PLAYING

7

Where Imagination Dwells

After Bob passed away, the future of his theater wasn't clear. No one had made plans for what to do when Bob was not there. The theater was important to the community, the families of Los Angeles, and the puppeteers. What would a world be like without Bob Baker's marionettes? Bob's staff was determined to keep the theater open, one day at a time. He had believed in his staff, and his staff believed in him. The age of puppeteers and artists in the workshop at this time was an important factor in this decision. Most of the employees were in their early twenties, and had come together and discovered a family—as well as a following for Bob and the puppets.

Living on borrowed time, the staff took advantage of every moment, every show, and every chance to celebrate the Bob Baker Marionette Theater. The first thing the staff decided to do was plan for a series of revivals of Bob's original shows that would rekindle the glory of the early theater years. Productions such as *The Sketchbook Revue*, *L.A. Olé!*, *The Circus*, and *The Enchanted Toyshop* were remounted over the next few years with an exuberance of youthful energy and enthusiasm.

In the first year after Bob's passing, the staff of the theater decided to host a public birthday party for him in February, as a celebration of his life and legacy. Bob always said he didn't want a funeral, so a birthday celebration was the obvious alternative. This marked a definitive moment in which the staff began to take ownership of the theater, and invest

Opposite: As the theater looked toward its future, renderings for a new space by Carson Brown helped develop a vision for their new home. Above: Bob Baker Day 2018.

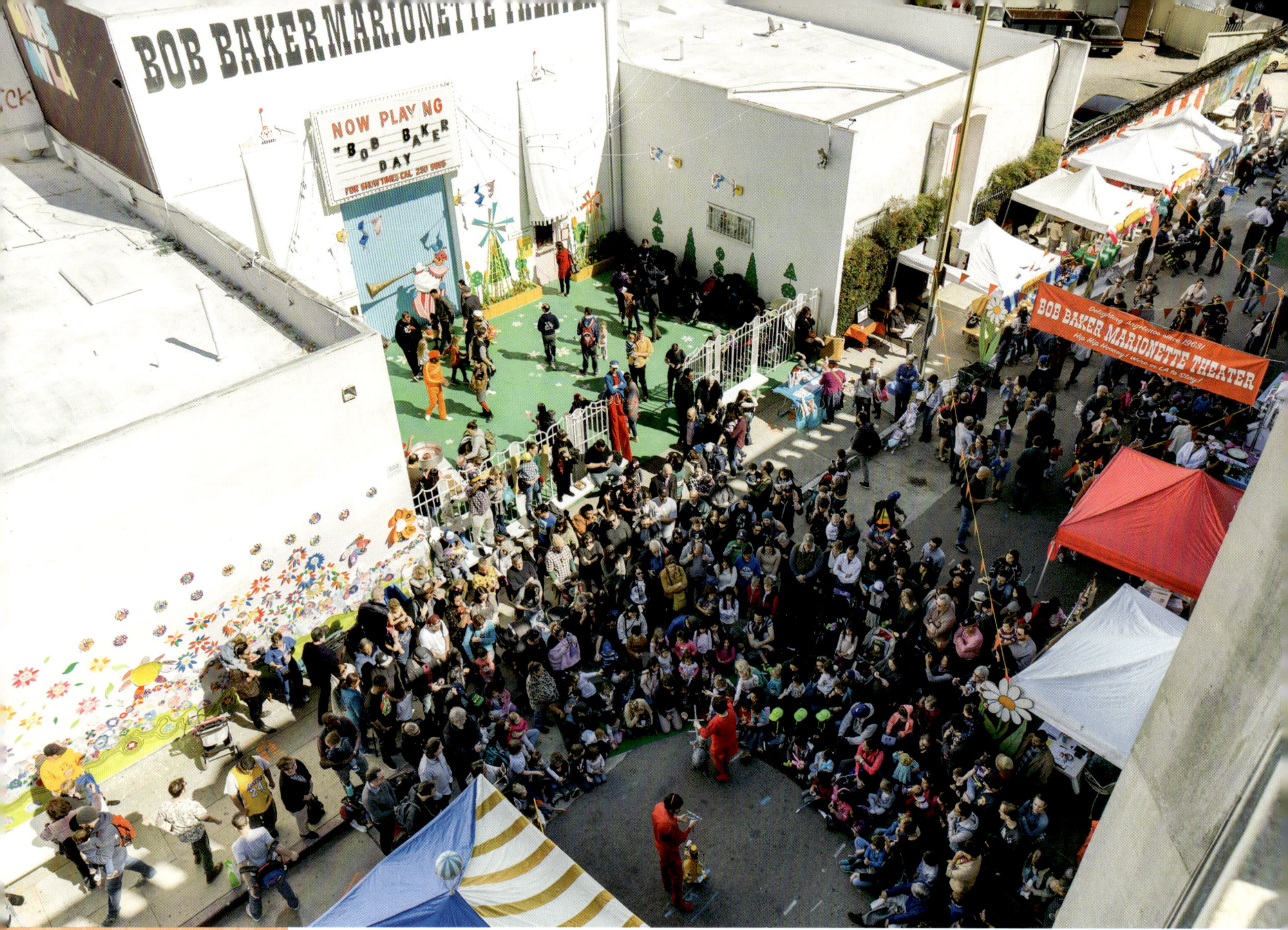

themselves in its continuation. They called the event "Bob Baker Day," and volunteers came together to repaint the courtyard patio of the theater, replace torn ornaments, and, for the first time in many years, restore "Toot," Bob's herald clown, to his proper place at the theater's entrance doors. The theater opened its doors to the community and celebrated every aspect of the world of Bob Baker: the music, the puppets, the art, and—most importantly—the people behind the theater. Old fans and new friends came into the space, and the connections that were made were so meaningful that Bob Baker Day became an annual tradition.

Bob once called his business "the most no-profit for-profit thing in the world." It turned out that he was right; the staff soon recognized the necessity of turning the theater from a business into a non-profit organization. By the end of 2016, Winona Bechtle began working with the theater as part of her master's degree program in arts management. She had been coming to see

marionette shows since she was five years old, and wanted to help the theater get on its feet. She helped the theater transition into a non-profit run by a team of staff led by Alex Evans, who would become the executive director. The Bob Baker Family Trust, headed by Bob's partner, Richard Schuler, would then allow all Bob's puppets and intellectual property—including the theater's library, recordings, and other documents—to be maintained by the new non-profit.

Bechtle's role quickly expanded to director of development and partnerships for the theater. As a non-profit, the theater's mission shifted to focus on service to the community. She tried to find creative ways to get people through the doors via a series of partnerships with arts organizations, hosting movie screenings, concerts, and other events that highlighted the theater's history.

As the Bob Baker Marionette Theater stabilized in the wake of Bob's passing, its staff and puppeteers began to plan for the future. It was one thing to just keep the theater running, but the staff wanted to move the theater into the future while maintaining continuity with the past. A group of staff puppeteers, designers, filmmakers, and Disney Imagineers came together to formalize the aesthetics and vision of the theater. They considered questions like "What makes a Bob Baker show?," asking how the theater saw itself, and how they wanted the public to see them. They codified their ideas into a document that specifically articulated what had once only been feelings and emotions. It suggested styles of artwork and design to be used for sets and puppets, as well as concepts and styles of writing for communications and poster design.

There was an outpouring of support from many young, talented volunteer artists and performers, all eager to make magic happen. The veteran puppeteers began to teach new puppeteers an art form that was dictated largely through oral history. The staff of puppeteers began holding

Top left: Staff and volunteers repair the original Calliope clown. Top right: Winona Bechtle carefully unpacks art from the Bob Baker archive while relocating the marionette concept art. Opposite: Bob Baker Day became a touchstone event for thousands of people in Los Angeles's creative community.

The stars of children's television sensation *Yo Gabba Gabba* pose in front of a mural by DABSMYLA (pictured center), helping to draw thousands of attendees to the second annual Bob Baker Day in 2016.

BOB
BAKER
MARIONETTE
THEATER

Spotlight on Talent

Braden Graeber

Braden Graeber saw his first Bob Baker show at age five. Years later, he returned to the theater to lend his talents to designing its posters and promotional materials. Graeber is responsible for re-creating the "feel" of the old Bob Baker theater at its new Highland Park location, working hard to blend the vintage Bob Baker look with modern styles. In addition to his work in advertising, Graeber became well-known for his creative contributions to internet culture.

regular meetings they called "Workshop Wednesdays," where they discussed Bob's artistry while reinvesting in the quality of the shows and puppeteer training. The Bob Baker staff was investing in a new generation of puppeteers the old-fashioned way. Those who had apprenticed with Bob were now training a younger generation in his unique style of puppetry.

Meanwhile, Eli Elimelech was still trying to figure out how to make his development work. The theater's staff had been banking on the idea that the landmark status would save them, because the designation was granted based on the association with the theater, not on the merits of the building itself. That is to say, without the Bob Baker Marionettes, the building never would have been a Historic-Cultural Monument. But they realized that, with only part of the building protected, they wouldn't be saved from eviction or remodeling. When the new renderings were unveiled, the staff discovered that a historic marker for the building would be displayed prominently, and pictures of puppets would be hung on that part of the structure—but that was all that would connect the building to its historic landmark status. "They're treating it like an architectural landmark," Evans said to the press, "but no . . . it's a cultural resource, and that's what's important."

The theater staff learned that developers were moving forward with the new apartment complex, without incorporating a functional space for the Bob Baker Marionette Theater into their plans. They wanted to build apartments on top of the theater, keeping the main performance area intact—but turning it into the lobby of the complex. The lobby would then feature puppet displays and a photographic

The process of packing up and moving the thousands of marionettes, pieces of artwork, and puppet-building materials led to the discovery of puppets and ephemera long believed lost forever.

exhibit of Bob's work. There would be no practical space dedicated to running the theater. The staff prepared for the worst, but never felt defeated. "If it shuts down tomorrow . . . it's horrible, but it's here right now, and it's going strong," Evans declared. "It's going to be as Bob wanted it to be. As long as we do a show tomorrow, Bob lives another day!"

They reached the end of the road in May 2018, when Elimelech announced that construction would begin on his project. He gave the puppeteers a ninety-day notice to vacate the premises. Despite being offered a chance to relocate to a smaller space inside the new complex, the team decided it was not a good option. Their finances had stabilized, the crowds had returned, and the puppets were more popular than ever. The theater needed to grow, and the only way to do that was to find a suitable new location. A small team led by technical director Kevin Beltz was dispatched to search surrounding properties for a new building. Before they were finished, the team had looked at more than thirty locations ranging from old warehouses, to theaters, to nondescript buildings. Evans encouraged the staff by announcing, "No matter how good the next place is, the real spirit of Bob Baker lives on in the puppets, strings, and costumes, and in the hands of the puppeteers that give them life. Wherever they are, Bob's legacy lives on. The magic will follow."

Spotlight on Talent

Kevin Beltz

Kevin Beltz, an award-winning designer and puppet fabricator, joined the Bob Baker Marionette Theater in 2018. Hired to help transition the company's performance infrastructure from its former Echo Park location to the new Highland Park theater, his considerable expertise has brought a renewed level of quality to the theater's second generation. Beltz also restores the vintage marionettes to their original perfection, and builds new puppets for new projects. He spent many years as a specialty prop builder. Beltz has used his skills of puppetry, animatronics, and theater design to create iconic props for some of television and film's largest spectacles, such as *Black Panther*, *Captain Marvel*, *The Muppets*, *Jurassic World*, and *Westworld*, to name a few.

The theater announced that the Bob Baker Marionettes would be moving by the end of the year. In honor of all the children who've loved the marionettes, they celebrated their last month in the Echo Park space by performing free shows for school groups. Their final show was scheduled for the day after Thanksgiving: November 23, 2018. It was timed exactly to the day that Bob first opened the theater in 1963, fifty-five years prior. After the show, they closed the theater's curtains for the final time, with no idea if they would ever have a permanent home again.

The theater's staff decided that if they couldn't be somewhere, they would have to be everywhere. They launched a vast series of road shows, residencies, and partnerships to bring the puppets out into the community. The staff had built up momentum,

Partnerships with Los Angeles State Historic Park (below), Occidental College (center), and Knott's Berry Farm (opposite) marked a renaissance of puppetry across a variety of Los Angeles institutions.

and didn't want to miss a beat. They took on the motto of "Imagination Dwells Here!"—the idea that the spirit of the Bob Baker Marionette Theater isn't bound up in the brick and mortar of the original location, but lives wherever the puppets dwell. Wherever the marionettes perform, imagination is sure to follow in abundance.

The day after closing, the Bob Baker Marionettes opened a successful five-week run of the theater's signature *Nutcracker* production at the historic Pasadena Playhouse. The team also mounted exhibits on puppetry for children's museums, and the puppeteers performed holiday road shows throughout the Christmas season. All of their hard work paid off; under the new management, the gross revenues from the theater nearly tripled. The theater's administrative expertise was greatly increased by the addition of many skilled volunteers. One in particular, Missy Steele, began her tenure by organizing the theater's archive of Disney-related material, and soon became the full-time director of operations, running the spotlight, booking field trips, and carting puppets and puppeteers all over Los Angeles.

In January of 2019, the theater finally found its new location. The new Bob Baker Marionette Theater would be located at 4949 York Boulevard in Highland Park. As fate would have it, the new theater was actually the former location of an old theater—the York Theatre, a former vaudeville and silent movie palace built in 1923. Over its almost hundred-year history, the building had also been home to the Korean Pyong Kang First Congregational Church of Highland Park, as well as an organ sales and repair store and a community barbershop. It was conveniently located across from a popular playground near Occidental College, in one of Los Angeles's most bustling neighborhoods. On February 15, Evans picked up the keys and signed the lease. "As Los Angeles experiences a time of change and development, the theater is energized to creatively seize the opportunity to grow as a cultural resource to educate, rejuvenate, and celebrate puppetry and the allied arts," the staff declared in a press release.

The first field trip in the new location with some very old puppets.

THE

"YORK THEATRE"

Announces
As It's Opening Date

Tuesday, September 18th

at 6:15 P. M.

The "York" is a Community Theatre
That Highland Park May Well Be Proud Of
Represents An Outlay of $100,000.
Strictly Modern in it's Appointments
$25,000. Big Wurlitzer Organ, Latest Model.
Leather Upholstered Opera Chairs Throughout
Seating Capacity 900

FIRST RUN PICTURES
HIGH CLASS VAUDEVILLE

OPENING NIGHT PROGRAM
Doors Open at 6:15

4--Big Vaudeville Acts--4

Direct From the Pantages Circuit

Leo Haley
The great Comedian. A Singing, Talking Act, coupled with imitations in "Gossip."

Gus Elmore & Co.
The wonder act, entitled "Circus Days." It's a scream from start to finish.

Noodles Fagan & Co.
In a new playlet entitled "A Vaudeville Surprise."

De Michele Bros.
Comedy Musical Act with Hoops, Violin and Harp. A big attraction.

ON THE SCREEN

"Hoot" Gibson in His New Picture **"Blinky"**

The new building had everything they wanted. The old theater had been 7,000 square feet; the Highland Park location would expand their space to 10,000 square feet. There was an opportunity to grow the business beyond just a puppet stage and party room—the theater team could now revisit some of Bob's earlier dreams about a puppet school and workshop. The new theater was a space with room not just for survival, but for growth. "In the new building, people can learn to paint, learn to sculpt," said Bechtle. "And we have open volunteer hours every week. There's a million and one ways where, even if you don't want to see a puppet, there are things you can do and get involved with."

Braden Graeber, the theater's design director, searched the archives for inspiration for the interior, carefully examining the original

Peeling back the layers of the York Theatre unearthed photographs, historic programs, and nearly a century of history that the Bob Baker team wanted to honor and preserve during construction. Below: Joel Freeman holds a chunk of the original theater wall; the new theater's walls were painted to match. Opposite: Even the chandeliers from the original theater made the move to the new location.

1007
SJIII 3219
1007

The return of commercial production in the new Bob Baker workshop began with a limited run of Bobo marionettes.

Ciro
ROSELAND
COLONIAL
The
BROWN
DERBY

Spotlight on Talent

Bob Breen

Bob Breen owns MorYork, the art collection and studio next door to the new Bob Baker Marionette Theater, with his husband, Clare Graham. Breen worked as an art director and set decorator in Hollywood for many years. He had no connection to the Bob Baker Marionettes before they arrived in the new location, but Breen was quickly swept up in the energy and excitement of the move. From the day the theater first unlocked its doors, Breen was lending a hand and adding his artwork to the space. He painted the theater's proscenium, curtain walls, and the dioramas inside the building. He also designed the "marionette mobile"—a mobile stage built inside a box truck the theater uses for road shows.

drawings created by Morton Haack and Serge Krizman. He made sure the new theater was built upon the dream of the old, keeping its most beloved and iconic elements while incorporating ideas Bob had developed, but never used.

Once the theater announced the move, more than 400 volunteers, including neighbors, friends, and even some former Disney Imagineers, came to help, assisting with cleaning, painting, and minor construction work. The Bob Baker staff had to do the heavier lifting—removing walls, designing designated spaces for artifacts, and hanging Bob's three gorgeous antique chandeliers—as well as building a metal structure to hold all of the puppets, curtains, and sets that were suspended backstage. As the boxes began to accumulate in the new location, the energy and spirit of the old theater began to fill the new space. By mid-July, the last puppet had been transferred to its new home, and the doors at 1345 West 1st Street were finally closed—with a sigh.

On November 29, 2019, one day to the year after the old location closed, the new Bob Baker Marionette Theater officially reopened. The staff held a day-long celebration, with free shows performed every half-hour to packed audiences. The staff felt that they had saved the theater, and wanted to share their hard work and joy with the community. Everyone had worried that some of the magic would be lost in the transition, but the generations of families in the audience—children, parents, and grandparents—embraced the theater and shyly, almost anxiously, whispered that the new location might, just might be even more special than the old.

Audrey Densmore and a Rhea bird marionette, which has been in active use at the theater for more than five decades. Though the audiences change and some of the performers come and go, the effect remains the same—delight, nostalgia, and charm will always be at the heart of the show.

12
3

Cristie Wilson's rendering of the new theater's lobby alongside the 1950s concept art for Disneyland's Tinkerbell Toy Shoppe window display. The purple-and-yellow jesters who graced the theater's old party room made the move to the new location. The new lobby space pays homage to these restored Disneyland artifacts, which were among the first projects Bob ever worked on at the park.

The York Theatre's original concession stand now sells puppets instead of popcorn for eager patrons to take home.

$10.00

Brendan Graber's concept sketch of the new proscenium is a hallmark of the theater's new look—drawing heavily from Morton Haack's original concept designs for the original location.

The proscenium, main performance space, and theater organ at the new home of the Bob Baker Marionette Theater.

A packed house welcomes the Bob Baker marionettes to their Highland Park theater on Grand Opening Day, November 29, 2019.

Afterword

The publication of this book marks one of the first occasions the theater has had to pause and take stock of its history. In looking back over the trials and triumphs of the last fifty-eight years, I'm reminded of a quote our facilities manager, Frank Fairfield, gave to the press as we were preparing to reopen the theater: "It's unlikely that we would work this hard to preserve a bunch of marionettes that are basically doing vaudeville. But here we are. It's so uncynical. It's imagination come to life. The York space used to be a vaudeville theater and a silent movie theater. Most recently it was a church. Alex and I were talking about how we have a kind of congregation here, gathered together in the name of imagination."

The Bob Baker Marionette Theater—our congregation of imagination—has drawn generations of people together, as artisans, as puppeteers, as staff, and as enraptured audiences caught up in the magic of marionettes. Our shows bring children into a conversation with artists and creators who worked years before those children were born—an aesthetic experience which ripples across time. Generations of families have enjoyed the theater: children grow older and bring their own children back for a puppet show, creating a culture and tradition that connects us to each other.

The theater resonates beyond a single puppet show or birthday party—its meaning comes from the community we create and the collective memories that we hold.

Just as a five-year-old Bob Baker saw an everyday show at a department store and discovered his life's calling, we offer the theater to the community in hopes that we may help another young child discover that same inspiration. At the end of every show, I tell the children and assembled audience that as a non-profit organization, the Bob Baker Marionette Theater is not our theater, it's their theater. When I look back over this collected history, I marvel at the generations of people who have gathered together under the banner of Bob's imagination. Now, as a reader of this book, you are part of the story, too.

Alex Evans

Executive Director and Head Puppeteer
Bob Baker Marionette Theater
2021

Alex Evans marvels at a trick puppet who grows a second head, crafted by four-year-old Julian.

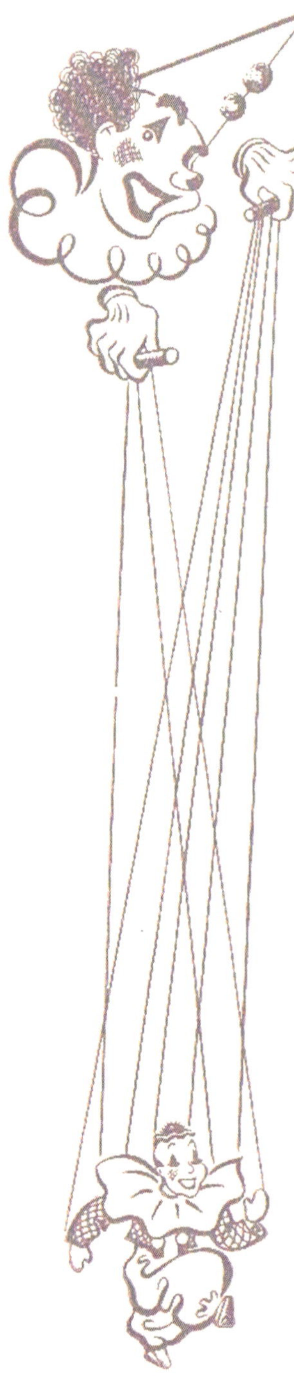

Acknowledgments

Randal J. Metz

Like the Bob Baker Marionette Theater, this book would not be as magical if not for the combined talents of so many folks behind the scenes. Each and every one of these people, in his or her own way, helped bring to life the history and artistry of Bob Baker and his theater. There were so many strings to pull on this one, so let's get started.

The talented staff of the Bob Baker Marionette Theater: A big thanks to Alex Evans and Winona Bechtle for their boundless help to make this book a reality. Extra special thanks to Elliot Kane, the awesome research archivist for the theater, who found answers to so many of the difficult questions. And special thank yous to Missy Steele, who helped with my endless calls, and Audrey Densmore, who reconnected me with the new Bob Baker Marionette Theater.

And, of course, the wonderful team at Angel City Press who believed in this project: Terri Accomazzo, our contact and editor for this tome, and J. Eric Lynxwiler for his fantastic graphic design work that added the "magical" touch to this book.

And many, many thanks to Jordan Peele for lending his voice to our puppet community.

An enormous thank you goes to Bob Baker historian Greg Williams, a master Bob Baker puppeteer himself, who kept alive the theater's history for others to enjoy. He also shared his personal knowledge and articles on Bob's history with the theater.

I also thank my good friend David Trice for helping me organize, research, and edit my thoughts during those long days combing through the Bob Baker archives.

Oh-so-many Bob Baker enthusiasts left their mark on this book through interviews, emails, and personal writings! That list includes Don Battjes, Tim Blaney, Tina Gainsboro, Ursula Heinle, John Leland, Ron Martin, Kevin Menegus, Bob Mills, Christine Papalexis, Richard Shuler, Charles Taylor, Allan Trautman, Tony Urbano, and René Zendejas.

A special thank you goes to the Los Angeles Public Library, who opened its Bob Baker photo collection and let me find just the right images to accompany my words. And speaking of images, this history would not be as beautiful as it is, without the talented group of photographers who supplied so many historical and promotional depictions illustrating life at the Bob Baker Marionette Theater.

Finally, I wish to thank Rhonda, who listened to all my ramblings and helped me untangle, understand, and manipulate Bob's fascinating legacy.

Bob Baker Marionette Theater

Bob Baker Marionette Theater would like to thank the following individuals and organizations:

Bob Baker & Alton Wood, without whom this vision would not exist. When we refer to "Bob and Alton", we also bring to mind the hundreds, if not thousands, of individuals who have contributed to the wonders that can be found in this book.

The man who has preserved and protected Bob's legacy: Richard Shuler.

Our foundation: Tina Gainsboro, Ursula Heine, and John Leland.

The theater's leaders, lovingly deemed "Bob's Bakers" who transitioned the theater into the future: Gary Baker, Winona Bechtle, Kevin Beltz, Joy Cho, Benjamin Dickow, Ginger Duncan, Mary Fagot, Colin Gibson, Danny Gonzalez, Vivian Gueler, Carrie Harr, Daisy Hernandez, Randy Lakeman, Gerg Maclaurin, Amy Minteer, Scott Moore, Chris and Charlene Nichols, Dante Ruiz, Peter Sattler, Missy Steele, and Jeptha Storm.

The team that saw us through our move to a new location and into the first few years of operation: Miguel Ayala, Ceylon Baginski, Bob Breen, Josh Briseno, Christine Casaus, Bill Crichton, Nic Cowan, Molly Cox Kathleen Craig, Eric De La Cruz, Karina De La Cruz, Audrey Densmore, Frank Escher, Suki-Rose Etter, Frank Fairfield, Molly Fite, Emily Frasu, Joel Freeman, Adam Foster, Adri Garcia, Natalia Gaydos, Ayrin Gharibpour, Ravi GuneWardena, Clare Graham, Seth Holmes, Joël Huxtable, Roxy Jamin, Elliot Kane, Fred Kolouch, Jed Lackritz, Megan Lee, Ilana Marks, Diego Montoya, Safowat Nazzal, Sasha Plotnikova, Jules O'Malley, Jamin Orrall, Mark H. Rhynes, Oscar Rosas, Carlos Sanchez, Dimitri Simakis, Caity Shaffer, Tomas Seidita, Kimmy Shields, Julian Small-Calvillo, Jeff Speetjens, Brianna Toth, Nova Trujillo, and Jared Whitham.

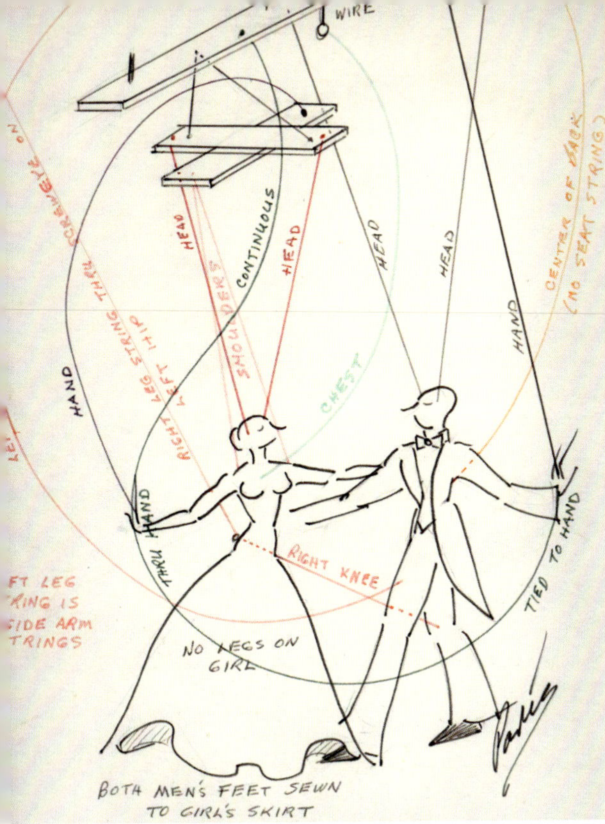

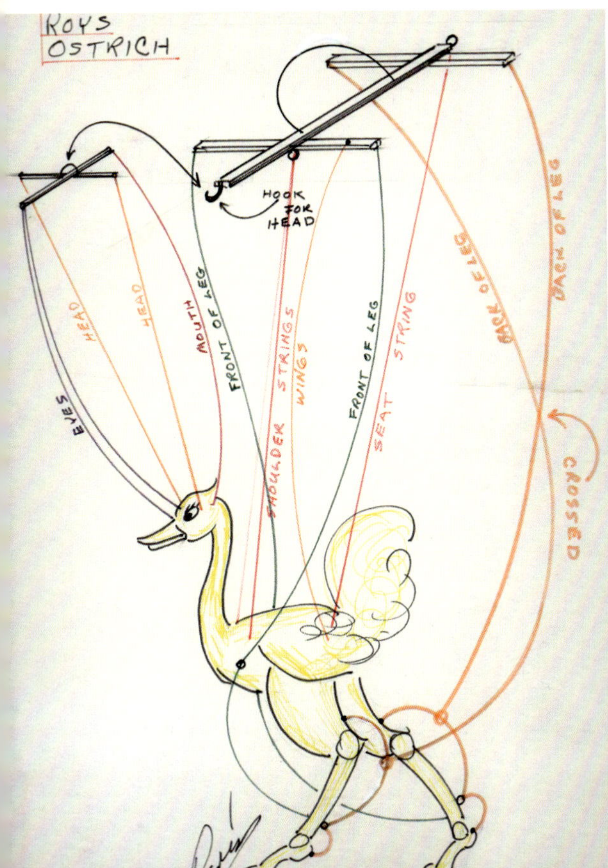

All the theater's staff, puppeteers, builders, and joy-givers: Ana Aguirre, Marina Aguirre, Jonathan Alvarez, Wilma Aquino, Martha Armstrong, Jerry Arnold, Mauri Bernstein, Zoe Brooke, Cain Carias, Scotty Castillo, Mary Ann Coria, Helen Crail, John Crawford, Velma Dawson, Ken Dodge, Suzanne Fergen, Peter Goldman, Morton Haack, King Hall, Sky Highchief, Teddy Lou Hikida, Ana Linares, Coral Kerr, Spencer King, Serge Krizman, Hoshiko Kusudo, Mirna Lissette, Juan Marroquin, Ron Martin, Adrian Martinez, Earl Montgomery, Lee Mosier, Victor Muñoz, Liz Nankin, Christine Papalexis, Sandi Price, Tom Ray, Roy Raymond, Don Sahlin, Mary Saxon, Anna Schaeffer, Matt Scott, Nicole Scott, Blanding Sloan, Dick Stoll, Thimbles the Theater Dog, James Trittipo, Oscar Weidhaas, Gregory Williams, Malcolm Wilkes, and René Zendejas.

Our passionate supporters, advisors, and friends: Harry Arrends, Carson Brown, Jane Canning, Chris Constable, Perry Daniel, Thom Fountain, Vanessa Gonzalez, Natalie Hadland, Rosalind Helfand, Alicia Houtrouw, Stephanie James, Nicholas Kasunic, Jordan Katz, Kaycee Krieg, Allison Krumwiede, Joe Lorge, Lori Meeker, Steve Meltzer, Rachel McDonald, Sabrina Parke, Julianna Parr, Beth Peterson, Charles Phoenix, Leslie Pruitt, Julie Roth, Lauren Scanlon, Rocky Schenck, Claire Vogel, Cristie Wilson, and Richard Wilson.

Our community of friends and organizations: Oscar Arce, David and Christina Arquette, The Armory Center for the Arts, Andrew Bakhit, Tony Baxter, Lindsay Benner, Big Bud Press, Tom Carroll, Alan Cook, The Core 24, Jody Daily, David Dastmalchian, DJ Lance Rock, Dublab, Dunn-Edwards Paint, Dynasty Typewriter, El Cine, Esotouric, Elena Flores, Forest Lawn Memorial-Parks, Steve Golden, Leslie Gray, LATOS, Los Angeles Breakfast Club, Los Angeles Guild of Puppetry, Kevin Kidney, Jennifer and Bert Klein, Eric Kurland, Le PeTiT CiRqUe, Ron Lynch, Brian Mikail, Jackee Marks, Museum of Jurassic Technology, Joanna Newsom, Tim Nordwind, Occidental College, Pasadena Playhouse, Santa Monica Pier, Mike Pearson, Aram Pogosian, Jean-Carlo Roncagliolo, Screen Novelties, Craig Sauer, Joe Selph, Negin Singh, Southern California Children's Museum, Tessa Tweet, TheatreDNA, Sara Velas, Greg Veneklasen, Vidiots, and Clay Westervelt.

The photographers and visual artists who captured our imagination: DABSMYLA, Dog Knit Sweater, Ian Byers-Gamber, Linnea Bullion, Shannon Korchinski, Mark Patricio, Roofless Painters, Stephenie Pashkowsky, Josh White, and Lisa Whiteman.

The puppeteers of tomorrow, including Dash, Colin, Julian, Rosie, Stephan, Uma, and Xavier.

Alta Dena Dairy, Balian Ice Cream, and wooden-spoon ice cream cups.

The Los Angeles Public Library and Christina Rice for preserving the Bob Baker Collection, and generously providing so many images for use in this book.

Endless thanks to our fearless leaders at Angel City Press—Terri Accomazzo and Paddy Calistro. Thank you for helping us share nearly a century of our history with friends and fans, both new and old. J. Eric Lynxwiler was stunningly adept at distilling decades of design into a book that truly feels like home to us.

Special thanks to Jordan Peele for contributing this book's foreword, and, finally, to our author and dear friend Randal J. Metz. Because of you, the voice of Bob and the theater is clearer than ever, and will resonate for generations to come.

"A wink of the eye, and a tip of the hat to all of you!"

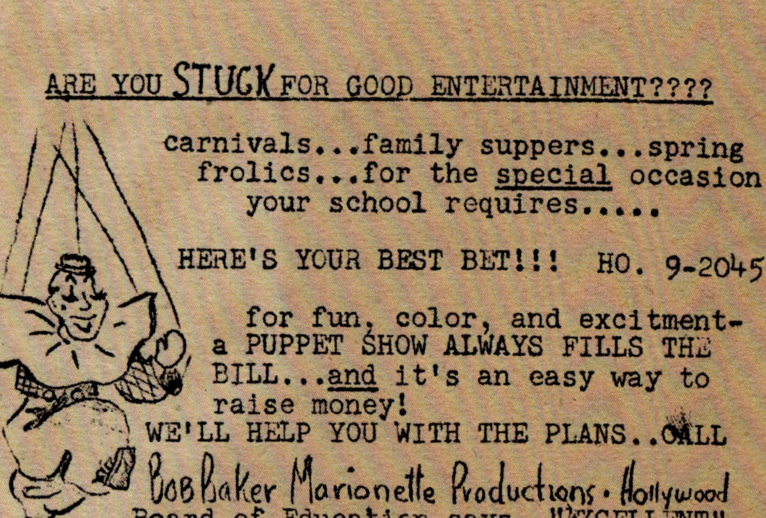

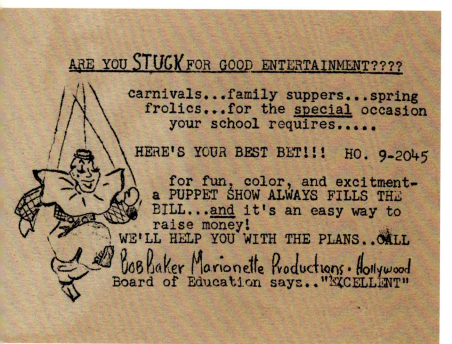

ARE YOU STUCK FOR GOOD ENTERTAINMENT????

carnivals...family suppers...spring frolics...for the special occasion your school requires.....

HERE'S YOUR BEST BET!!! HO. 9-2045

for fun, color, and excitment-a PUPPET SHOW ALWAYS FILLS THE BILL...and it's an easy way to raise money!
WE'LL HELP YOU WITH THE PLANS..CALL
Bob Baker Marionette Productions • Hollywood
Board of Education says.."EXCELLENT"

Author **Randal J. Metz** is the founder of The Puppet Company, based in the San Francisco Bay Area. He and puppet partner Rhonda Godwin perform shows throughout California. Since 1991, Randal has been the resident puppet master for The Storybook Puppet Theater at Children's Fairyland in Oakland. The Storybook Puppet Theater is the oldest continuously running puppet theater in the United States. Metz has authored several history books on Fairyland and the history of puppetry in California.

Designer **J. Eric Lynxwiler** first visited the Bob Baker Marionette Theater in the first grade, which cemented his love of puppetry for a lifetime. He has written three books for Angel City Press on Wilshire Boulevard, Knott's Berry Farm, and neon signs, and has designed and researched images for numerous other titles on aspects of Southern California history.

Photo Credits All images are from the Bob Baker Marionette Theater archives except as noted here: Alamy: 111 • AP: 104 (bottom left) • Oscar Arce: 148 • Artists Association Nantucket: 22 (top) • Eric Axene: 14 • Ian Byers-Gamber: cover, 82 (left, right), 83 (top left, top right), 127, 135, 146, 152 (right), 153 (right), 158, 164, 168 • Nolwen Cifuentes: 161 • J. Emilio Flores: 6 • Natalie Hadland 170, 172 • Christian Hynes: 141 • KHM-Museumsverband, Theatermuseum Vienna: 22 (middle) • J. Eric Lynxwiler: 26, 92–93 (all), 95 • Los Angeles Public Library, Bob Baker Collection: 2, 8, 16, 17, 18, 20 (all), 21, 23, 24 (all), 29 (all), 31 (all), 32 (bottom), 34, 35, 38, 41 (bottom left), 41 (bottom right), 44, 47 (bottom), 49 (bottom), 49 (top), 50 (left), 51, 52, 53 (all), 56 (top), 57, 58, 59 (all), 60 (right), 61, 63 (top), 65, 66 (all), 67 (all), 72, 75, 76 (all), 77, 82, 83 (bottom), 84, 87, 89 (bottom left, bottom right, middle left, top left), 90, 99, 102 (all), 103, 104 (bottom left, top left), 108 (right), 109 (bottom), 115, 116 (all), 117 (all), 124, 129 (all), 132 (all), 133, 134, 135 • Los Angeles Public Library, Yale Puppeteers & Turnabout Theatre Collection: 22 (bottom) • Randal J. Metz: 12, 13 • Tony Overman: 110 • Oxy Arts: 153 (left) • Pacific Union Recorder: 156 (top left) • Stephenie Pashkowsky: 11 • The Puppetry Journal: 138 • Rocky Schenck: 140 • Carrie Schreck: 145 • Ryan Schude: 142-143 • Joe Selph: 28 • Charles Taylor: 113 (all)• Claire Marie Vogel: 89 (top right) • Richard Vogel: 121 (bottom) • Lisa Whiteman: 139, 150, 151, 168, 172

Enchanted Strings: Bob Baker Marionette Theater

By Randal J. Metz
Foreword by Jordan Peele

Design by J. Eric Lynxwiler, Signpost Graphics

10 9 8 7 6 5 4 3 2 1

ISBN 978-1-62640-107-5

Library of Congress Cataloging-in-Publication Data is available.

Published by Angel City Press
www.angelcitypress.com

Printed in Canada